WHAT BOTHERS US ABOUT GROWNUPS

WHAT BOTHERS US

ABOUT GROWNUPS

A REPORT CARD ON ADULTS BY CHILDREN
EDITED BY RUSSEL HAMILTON AND STEPHANIE GREENE
THE STEPHEN GREENE PRESS * BRATTLEBORO

Dedication: to eight-to-twelve-year-olds everywhere—and their grownups

This book has been manufactured in the United States of America: designed by Russel Hamilton, composed on IBM Selectric Composer, Type 6151, in IBM Century and Univers types, printed by The Vermont Printing Company and bound by The Book Press. It is published by The Stephen Greene Press, Brattleboro, Vermont 05301

Library of Congress Catalog Card Number: 68-54446
International Standard Book Number: 0-8289-0086-8

CONTENTS

... to tell me when your book is done. I might want to by whom. address 32 South S

INTRODUCTION

who is writing the book?

About the Editors:

STEPHANIE GREENE is the daughter of Stephen and Janet Greene, the President and Editor-in-Chief respectively of The Stephen Greene Press, and it is on Stephanie's initiative that there *is* a *What Bothers Us about Grownups*. The idea germinated in a parent-child conversation recollected to have been about as follows:

Daughter: You know what I'll never do as a grownup?

Father: No, what?

Daughter: I'll never be rude to kids. They can't be rude back.

Father: That's so, but how many parents remember it? I used to have a list of things I promised myself I'd never do as a grownup, but I've forgotten everything on it except that I vowed I'd never say, "My, how you've grown!" to a child. I automatically hated any grownup who pulled that one on me.

Daughter: You've never said it to me. What about telling the same joke 1,000 times? [*Pause*] Do you think any grownups remember their childhood "pet peeves?"

Father: Probably not. It would be interesting to know . . .

The upshot was that Stephanie soon made a list of her own of "what I won't do to kids when I grow up!" from which point the notion to attempt a book of this nature took root.

Stephanie had just turned 13 when this took place and, having witnessed considerable editorial *Sturm und Drang* already, was resolved *never* to be an editor in later life.

Be that as it may, she has meanwhile edited effectively in making *What Bothers Us about Grownups* the book it is, cheerfully sacrificing much vacation time to the selection of questionnaires for reproduction and quotation and to the often frustrating task of sorting and classification, the "sheer handling" of a bulky mass of paper. In addition to performing this drudgery, she continually warned the elder editor against getting too wound up; so that he might fail to distinguish between, for example, a child's complaint about a beating (as personal experience) and *beating* (as a thing *not* to do). Stephanie more than once enabled her doddering colleague of 50-plus years to time-travel back to age 13.

RUSSEL HAMILTON remembers his childhood as a time of always having to go to bed too soon, and of trying to cope with lettuce, one of Satan's tools for creating parent-child discord at table. (Lettuce is unmanageable until full manual coordination has been achieved, Mom.)

Hamilton worked for five years as counselor at a summer camp for boys, achieving popularity once a week by distributing the campers' spending-money allowances. Following college, he worked in an advertising agency specializing in book publishers' accounts. In this capacity, and as proprietor of his own home-based agency, he has prepared copy for hundreds of childrens' books, notably the original Babar books, the enchanting Betsy-Tacy stories by Maud Hart Lovelace, and the highly regarded First Books series. One agency-client relationship lasting 25 years was with one of America's preeminent publishers of juveniles.

He has written, edited, compiled, and illustrated some half-dozen books for young readers. These include two First Books [*Trains* and *Photography*, 1954 edition] at the *What Bothers Us about Grownups* reading level, and *Science, Science, Science* for junior high readers up.

Russ Hamilton's own brood numbers a son and two daughters. They have forfeited — by growing up — their *What Bothers Us* questionnaire opportunity to zero in on mom and dad. But their reading of many of the replies has been punctuated by many *now*-you-know asides. Hamiltons *mère* and *père* are gratified at the apparent willingness, and even eagerness, with which from time to time their young ones return to the roost from somewhat inconveniently distant walks of life. Is it because we did something right during their formative years? Or because — Marge Hamilton is a good cook!

QUESTIONNAIRE FOR BOYS AND GIRLS

We know that there are a lot of things that we grownups do and say that
bother or embarrass you. We'd like to know what these things are. Please
answer these questions:

List the things that bother you most about grown-ups!

a)_____

b)_____

c)_____

List three things you will always remember to do around children when you
grow up.

a)_____

b)_____

c)_____

List three things you

a)_____

b)_____

c)_____

List three things that

a)_____

b)_____

c)_____

Any further comments?

_____

_____

_____

Your Town:_____
Are you a boy?_____

Please return this she

Book Publishers

THE STEPHEN GREENE PRESS

120 Main Street · BRATTLEBORO, VERMONT

Dear Teacher;

      This is an experiment, one on which we would like your help.

      I think we all remember that as children we made resolves that
we would--or would not as the case might be--do certain things when we
grew up to be adults. These resolves were based of course on experiences,
both pleasant and unpleasant, with our elders.

      I have forgotten entirely what I was firmly determined 45 years
ago not to forget. So this experiment is an attempt to recall these
things through the experience of today's children. A book will come of
it perhaps.

      We have devised a questionnaire which we would like as many
children as possible in the third through the sixth grades to fill out.

      The first draft of this questionnaire included sample answers,
but these have been deleted on the theory that the children would be
guided too closely by the illustrations and would not do their own thinking. However, some examples might be useful in explaining to the children
what we are looking for. So here they are.

    (List the things that bother you most about grown ups.) <u>Example</u>:
THEY TALK TOO MUCH.

    (List three things you will always remember to do around children
when you grow up.) <u>Example</u>: TALK <u>TO</u> KIDS, RATHER THAN ABOUT
THEM.

    (List three things you promise you won't say or do to kids when you
grow up.) <u>Example</u>: COMMENT, ON MEETING, "MY HOW YOU HAVE
GROWN!"

    (List three things that really trouble you about being a child.)
<u>Example</u>: HAVING TO WASH ALL THE TIME.

      I know you can think of some better examples than this.

      Thanks so much for your help.

               Sincerely,

               Stephen Greene

The questionnaire and its accompanying letter to schoolteachers

CHAPTER I

THE "WHAT BOTHERS US" QUESTIONNAIRE AND ITS DISTRIBUTION

I hate nosy idiots
like you who give
us questionnaires

I want to be a teacher
for 4th grade. I hope
to give out things
like this.

TIME: mid-Spring, 1968. Decision made: to attempt a book exploring children's chief grievances against adults now, and the corollary, how they propose to behave toward children when they grow up.

To get data from the children, a questionnaire appeared to be just the thing (such a grown-up solution!). Harder to think through was *what* to ask, then *how* to ask it so that the kids would answer frankly, in their own words. A third problem would be how to get a *quantity* of answers in reasonably swift time. The complication here was that if we were to work through the schools, as seemed most feasible, the school year was running out.

While at work on the first two items, we wrote to friends active in various school systems across the country, and were heartened by replies promising ready and eager cooperation in whatever we decided to do.

With the help of Dorothy A. Cole, Ph.D., psychologist at the Brattleboro Family and Child Guidance Services, Inc., we prepared a questionnaire that our educator friends could circulate in their classrooms. That this should be aimed at the middle grades seemed best, to be sure of a degree of articulateness in the children's answers and at the same time keep clear of the ages at which boys and girls begin to "think teen," or even to have taken on some adult coloring.

Shown opposite are the questionnaire and accompanying letter which went out first to various Vermont schools. In later, farther-flung distributions, we changed the heading to read simply, QUESTIONNAIRE FOR BOYS AND GIRLS. The "questions" were worded as follows:

1. List the things that bother you most about grownups.
2. List three things you will always remember to do around children when you grow up.
3. List three things you promise you won't say or do to kids when you grow up.
4. List three things which really trouble you about being a child.
5. Any further comments?

Also added, below the "Your Town" line, were the queries "Are you a boy? . . . Or girl?" when it became evident from the initial response that the youngsters wouldn't say unless asked. Furthermore, a random reading of the responses from nearby schools showed, for the most part, that we couldn't tell whether a boy or a girl was speaking!

Perhaps this was a statistical boner. In our desire to put the boys and girls at ease, completely anonymous and unfettered in their answering, we never considered that a sex differentiation might more sharply illuminate the reading and interpretation of the answers.

In the end, we accumulated enough definite boy-or-girl indications to show, as Editor Greene maintains, that the boys in general tend to zero in on things with more determination and vehemence than the girls do, whereas the sexes are virtually united in detail on "what bothers us about grownups."

What Our Teacher Friends Said

AS YET undecided was the question: to publish or not to publish? Without a body of material at hand, how could we decide? Perhaps we'd asked silly questions and would get silly answers. Then the neighborhood and countryside began to respond. A batch from Brattleboro. Some from upstate. A hundred or so more in the next mail. Soon, with nearly all our Vermont people heard from, we had a box full of questionnaires—from which we reproduce in this chapter a number of the ones that influenced us to go ahead. You see them exactly as we did, except for the school, teacher, name, and address information we promised to keep confidential.

Allowing for transcontinental mail schedules and the various schools' programming convenience, it took somewhat over three months to accumulate the more than 1,200 filled-out questionnaires from which this book has been made.

The publisher and editors gratefully acknowledge herewith the assistance of all the cooperating school personnel on whom we imposed the traffic burden of distribution, collection, and follow-through in the classrooms.

Some of the teachers took time out of their crowded year-end schedules to write . . .

" . . . got a request from a school principal here for 350 *more* of your forms! He doesn't want only some of his classes to fill them out . . . Hope the project is getting places. The children seem to enjoy the outlet for their frustrations. What can you do for adults?" [*Source:* Midwest]

" . . . it has been fun—the kids loved expressing themselves on this subject— and one Fifth Grade teacher saved a copy to use next year." [West Coast]

"Don't dispare! (as the kids would write it.) The forms are on their way. I trust they are not too late, as there are three or four real gems . . .

"In spite of evidence to the contrary, we do teach spelling here!

"This is really a great idea, and I hope you go through with your plans to publish your findings. Actually, there is a certain ambivalence in my feelings as I go over the answers; some of them are very funny, at the same time there is a sadness that underlies many of the replies. It could serve as a good text for parents to evaluate what they are doing to their children.

"I'm glad you 'included us in'." [West Coast]

"Your book on children's views is a superb idea . . . Will return forms to you as soon as they are back. Have tried to get some [*name of school deleted*] ghetto kids, which should be interesting." [New England]

" . . . asked me to send these to you. Hope they're helpful. Found them fascinating myself!" [Eastern state]

What Some of the Children Said

THE CHILDREN'S own opinions were eagerly sought—and easily found—in Section 5 of the forms: *Any further comments?*

I think this is fun and HARD.
yes I thought is was fun this paper.
its stupid!
It made me think! It^{was}very much fun! But it^{was}very hard!
i t s s i l l y
its hard
It's funny

That was Third Grade speaking. To continue on up the grades . . .

Why do we have to do all these things I tryed to answer all of them crocly.

I think this is the best idea since my father thought of going camping. Thank you for asking us.

No. But I think that was good thinking of doing this.

Why did we have to do this sheet? It is riduillous.

Yes! I want to be a teacher when I grow up. I want to be a teacher for 4th grade. I hope to give out things like this.

Yes. Well I like the idea of writing a book to show the feelings of children over grown-ups

Yes who is Mr. Green.

wy do want to know for

Why didn't you have us put are names on this sheet?

yes Why do you want theas.

I think this is the silliest thing I've ever heard of. Why do you ask such crazy questions?

And now, Grade Five . . .

Yeah.   Thanks, S. Greene

I hope this book is a good success.

I think you were being rather personal, however I tried to help you with your book by answering the questions

I think it was a good idea of yours to ask children around the country to answer these questions

I don't like this becuse it tells all my secrets away

Yes. I told Mrs T------- that I would like a book when it came out.

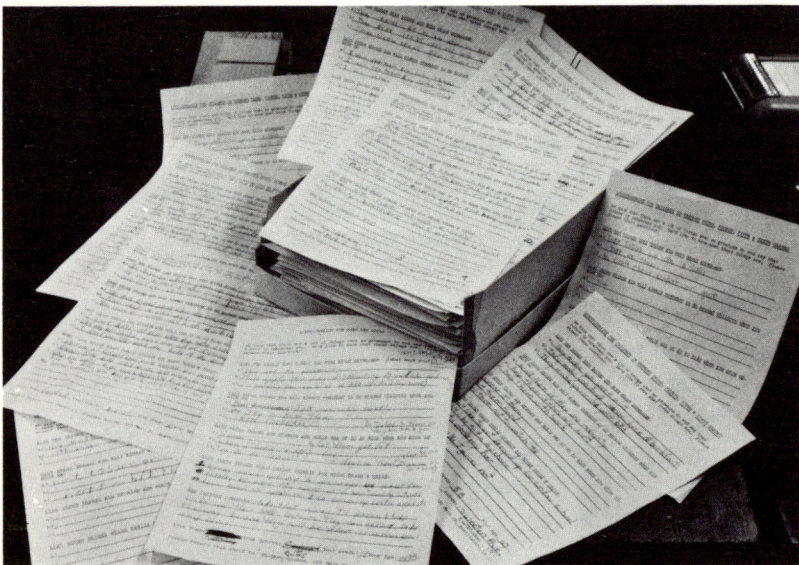

Editor's-eye-view of the accumulating questionnaires

QUESTIONNAIRE FOR CHILDREN IN VERMONT
THIRD, FOURTH, FIFTH & SIXTH GRADES

We know that there are a lot of things that we grownups do and say that bother or embarrass you. We'd like to know what these things are. Please answer these questions:

List the things that bother you most about grown-ups.

a) They neve talk to you,

b) They are good to children,

c) They are talking all the time

List three things you will always remember to do around children when you grow up.

a) I will not lie to my children

b) Children shauld

c) Make children mind,

List three things you promise you won't say or do to kids when you grow up.

a) I promise not to _____ them,

b) I promise to be nice to children,

c) I promise to love _____.

List three things which really trouble you about being a child.

a) I wish I were out of schl.

b) I wish I were a teacher,

c) I wish I were a millionare,

Any further comments? Yes I thought is was fun this paper

Your School: _____ Your Grade: 3 Your Age: 9

5

QUESTIONNAIRE FOR BOYS AND GIRLS

We know that there are a lot of things that we grownups do and say that
bother or embarrass you. We'd like to know what these things are. Please
answer these questions:

List the things that bother you most about grown-ups.

a) _When my father smokes._

b) _____

c) _____

List three things you will always remember to do around children when you
grow up.

a) _Do not say bad words._

b) _____

c) _____

List three things you promise you won't say or do to kids when you grow up.

a) _I won't kill them._

b) _____

c) _____

List three things which really trouble you about being a child.

a) _I want to be 21 years old._

b) _____

c) _____

Any further comments? _I do not want to
go to war._

Your School: _____ Your Grade: _5 B_ Your Age: _10_

6

Yes Mr. H------ I will not answer your question But I don't think yow showld get in other people's afair over ➔ and how do we know what we are go to do tell we grow up and Why are you asking these question? Well I don't know why but I not going to answerned them maybe someone will but I not

And she didn't! But a classmate of hers did, before having this to say . . .

Yes. Why do you ask these questions? You have to interfear in peoples business doen't you. I doen't see why you should. You just <u>over</u> want to find out if children like there parents. Well I love my parents and you aren't going to find out mutch from me.

Ladies, please! Stop browbeating us bewildered grownups. May you both have to make out your own Income Tax Returns!

I thought these were good questions. And I wish you were always a grown-up.

This was kind of hard for me because there isn't much that bothers me about grownups

I would like to know what this is for.

I've always wanted to say this. (Especially when I'm mad at mom + DAD.

Why do we have to do this for you people ?????? Please tell me the answer.

I hope you have success with your project!

No but (I wish you luck on your book.)

At this point Fifth Grade gives way to Sixth . . .

I believe that these are the hardest questions I've ever tried to answer.

Thanks for leting us express our feelings because grown-ups never care what kids think.

N̶O̶ h̶e̶ tell me when your book is done I might want to by whon.

I think this is nutty.

Thank you for asking these questions.

I hope something will become of this ! ! !

This is rediculious

When you print the book would you please send me a copy.

N̶o̶ Yes, I enjoyed this very much.

To be quite honest with you, this is kind of hard to answer, but I tried my best, some things I never thought of before.

It troubles me to have little questionnaires and silly questions

Yes, I hate grownups who yell at the child. They only make the child made at you. I also hate nosy idiots like you who give us questionaires

Here the children's comments on the subject ceased, we thought. And then, from a Miss 11 in Fifth Grade . . .

List the things that bother you most about grownups.
a)   **My parents say I eat as many potatoes as a mouse**
b)   **My parents don't let me stay up any later than**
c)   **And that (You People) made me do 9:00 THIS!**

This final, emphatic heckling couldn't curdle the fact that, of the boys and girls who *did* take the trouble to comment, more than half were positively *for* the idea. These sentiments, the teachers' enthusiasm, and our own inclination decided us to go ahead with a book based on the returned questionnaires.

NORTHEAST   MIDWEST   WEST COAST
The questionnaires arranged according to regional source

We worried briefly that our 1,000-odd replies weren't enough really to tell what kids (as a population) think about grownups. We were comforted by remembering that the Nielsen thunderbolts stem from what most people consider to be a surprisingly small sample.

Also, what about that largest pile of forms returned just from northeastern America? Would this regional preponderance spoil the consensus? To settle this matter we set aside the locals, temporarily, to listen to the boys and girls from "away." Apart from an Age 10 out West who is specifically annoyed by **aunts from Massachusetts**, what-bothers-us-about-grownups comes up the same with little regard to the locale where you happen to be growing up.

No child in any time zone wants to go to bed at an hour he considers to to be too soon. Not one of them anywhere praises the native produce—eggplant, broccoli, spinach, cauliflower—in gourmet terms if it has been force-fed by adult command. With grownups the way they are, there is little difference

8

of note anywhere, anytime, according to these experts.

Having calmed our misgivings, we stacked up our 1,226-page, handwritten manuscript and prepared to tune in on what the you-should-be-seen-but-not-heard crowd has to say.

List the things that bother you most about grown-ups.

1) _Yell at you_   4. _Make you go to bed early_
2) _Talk privately_   5. _Make you stay home from school_
3) _Make you eat brusell sprouts_   6. _They tell who your boyfriend is_

List three things you will always remember to do around children when you grow up.

1) _I will play with them_   4. _I will not smoke_
2) _I will set a good example_
3) _and I won't make them eat brussel sprouts_

List three things you promise you won't say or do to kids when you grow up.

1) _I will not sware_
2) _I will not smoke_
3) _I will not drink L.S.D._

List three things which really trouble you about being a child.

1) _having to play with someone you don't like_
2) _having a terrible sister_
3) _going to the store_

Any further comments? _I would like to say that these things I wrote down are not made up I hate brussells sprouts_

Your School: _____ Your Grade: _6_ Your Age: _11½_

9

List the things that bother you most about grown-ups.

a)_____

b)_____

c)_____

List three things you will always remember to do around children when you grow up.

a)_____

b)_____

c)_____

List three things you promise you won't say or do to kids when you grow up

a)_____

b)_____

c)_____

List three things which really trouble you about being a child.

a) Because I have serablepalsu

b)_____

c)_____

Any further comments? NO _____

_____

_____

Your School:_____ Your Grade: 6   Your Age: 11

10

CHAPTER II

PROCESSING THE QUESTIONNAIRES

Please return this sheet to: Stephen Greene, Br*we will*,

OPTIMISTICALLY we announced *What Bothers Us about Grownups* in our Fall catalog and turned to the work of making a readable book out of a potential 18,930 lines of comment on adults by children. In typical, organized adult fashion one of us presumed that the kids would say straight off, on line *a)* of Question 1, THE thing that bothers them most about grownups. Instant interpretation; what could be simpler? And quick, too.

In very short order, this editor was reduced to the state of mind of a Den Mother shepherding her Cubs in Fenway Park on Children's Day at the ball game.

Also, he found himself entertained, delighted, informed, and refreshed by the *vitality* of these young ones welling up from handwriting of every describable quality (except, perhaps, Spencerian). Here were whoops and hollers, shouts and murmurs, catcalls and chatter emanating from a burgeoning energy that, alas, will all too soon settle into the comfortable, dull power of maturity. What a reminder for grownups of a state of being never to be relived, and that once drove them relentlessly toward being—grown up!

However, there was one of America's top-notch medics at hand to steady him—or any adult whose association with children in quantity stirs up a whirl of emotion and nerves. Dr. Henry A. Schroeder, medical scientist, teacher, and respected authority on heart disease and hypertension, reminds us (in a book that ranges the spectrum of human relations, including health†)

---

† "A Matter of Choice." 1968, Brattleboro, The Stephen Greene Press. Quoted by permission of the author.

that ". . . for the first ten years or so, you were a selfish little animal, grabbing, scrabbling, fighting—living only in your own limited world more or less instinctively, demanding, crying when your immediate wants were not immediately granted—on the emotional level of a somewhat less than intelligent monkey. Imposed on this selfishness were the disciplines of your environment: the wills of your parents, the opposing demands of your brothers and sisters and of your herd of little animals, the weather, and other numerous restrictions essential to your health and your survival . . . During this period you had few

List the things that bother you most about grown-ups.

a) They sit on the toilet all day long.

b) They tease me about my boyfriends

c) The don't like fun.

List three things you will always remember to do around children when you grow up.

a) (be giving)!   (and not my dumb way

b) let them have their own way if it is sensible

c)

List three things you promise you won't say or do to kids when you grow up.

a)

b)

c)

List three things which really trouble you about being a child.

a) Not allowed to Ride bikes or hoses on the main

b) Road

c)

Any further comments? I don't like this becaus it Tells all my secrets away

Your Grade: D   Your Age: 10

12

List the things that bother you most about grown-ups.

a) _Smoking._

b) _When you talked) to theum they don't listen_

c) _When you tell them you would like to meet a girl they blab it_

List three things you will always remember to do around children when you grow up.

a) _always listen to them_

b) _____

c) _____

List three things you promise you won't say or do to kids when you grow up.

a) (promising) I won't (scream) literate (I don know how to spell it)

b) _____

c) _____

List three things which really trouble you about being a child.

a) _____

b) _____

c) _____

Any further comments) _this is about 1.L. they asplashlee tell the girls mother._

Your School: _____ Your Grade: _5 B_ Your Age: _12_

free choices." You also had (remember?) a "tough, self-centered little psyche."

Nevertheless, as a starting point, an exploration of the children's answers to line a) of Question 1 seemed satisfactory. We shuffled the deck, so to speak, and went through it noting every tenth reply. From this 10 percent sampling we hoped for a directive. What we got was what we might have guessed at, based on Dr. Schroeder's wisdom. What bothers kids most about grownups—about anything?— boils down to RESTRICTION ...

13

Grown - ups. are to bossy
They make you practice playing the oargan
My brother sits on me too much
They make you go to bed when your not tired
they boss us around
I can ' t go up town.
they won't let you watch T.V. when you want to
Always think they're the boss
They Boss you around to much.
You can't do what you want to do
When they say your to young to watch a monster movie
When they tell you not to bother your sister when shes buging you
I get tired of them always ordering me around
They're always saying do this, do that
They don't let you do much by yourself

and
they
know
it

. . . and so on. Almost coequal with restriction was NOISE, adult-type noise as
distinguished from noise they make themselves.

They yell at me
They bother me by yelling at me.
they scream too much.
They yell at you when you don't do anything wrong
They holler at you.
There always screaming at you for no reason at all
They are always yelling all the the times.
Yelling at you for no reason
Their yelling sometimes.

Thus the children were telling us at a glance what we should already
have known: they object to grownups' noisy omnipotence. Doesn't everybody?

But among those first-off first lines were other shades of opinion . . .

They think they are bbig.
they are sametime g r o u c h y
I try to make someone happy and somebody gets angry at me
They are haircut happy. All they do is cut our hair
They always tease you about the person you like
?!@†?*!! 1.a Well they give you lecters and try to make you just perfect
Why do they drink beer and rome?
Some how I have a feeling a few of my aunts and uncles don't like me
When they fight
They said bad wrods
When they s mok and blow it in your face

QUESTIONNAIRE FOR BOYS AND GIRLS

We know that there are a lot of things that we grownups do and say that
bother or embarrass you. We'd like to know what these things are. Please
answer these questions:

List the things that bother you most about grown-ups.

a) _When I have a friend down they alway bawl me_
b) _When my little brother or sister gets hurt_
c) _When my favorite T.V. program comes_

List three things you will always remember to do around children when you
grow up.

a) _Let them watch their favorite progra_
b) _When they ask me a question on →_
c) _Give them a reward if they do a →_

List three things you promise you won't say or do to kids when you grow up.

a) _I won't punish him until I hear their_
b) _Never tell them to go out while compan_
c) _Never tell them to do this + that →_

List three things that really trouble you about being a child.

a) _Nobody ever listens to you and trys t_
b) _They always shout "No" to you →_
c) _They always say, "You're been →_

Any further comments? _No_

_____
_____
_____

Your Town: Your School: Your Grade: 6 Your Age: 11
Are you a boy?_____   Or Girl? ✓

Not enough room to complain? Just flop the sheet over . . .

A. out in front of her.
B. they bawl me out even if I wasn't even around.
C. on My Mother always turns it to something really dull

2. B. homework I'll never give them a big long lecture on how you should listen to the teacher.

2.C chore,

3.A part of the story,
B. visiting.
3C. at your birthday party.

4.A understand why you did it.
4.B. When you ask them something
4C. talking on that phone for an hour," when it's only been 10 min.

. . . and carry on!

My Mother always gets mad it me when one of my sisters do it.
They tell you what they think is right but you can't tell them what

. . . which last echoes Editor Greene's original premise: "Kids can't be rude back." (See Introduction.)

So there was to be no quick, easy way to The Message, if any. We would be better advised to let the kids do the talking, and, should something conclusive emerge, let it be determined by consensus, or "the sense of the meeting." In the mass, our authors might be "typical" but individually they refused to be "standard."

This, of course, *did* involve sorting, selection, classification, and tabulalation, but hardly with the whirlwind efficiency of a computer analyzing a thousand sets of fingerprints.

The distractions were too delightful. Shown on following pages are two forms from Fifth Grade, one a lucid, down-the-line statement of opinion in which swearing tops all. The other is—well the young man dislikes that he's bossed around and that he can't talk back to grownups, but then his report sort of disorganizes itself into a special situation unique to our group. *This* is the kind of response that kept blurring the statistics and made us feel that we would do the kids a disservice merely by tabulating them. (Who wants to be a statistic, at any age?)

Therefore the meat of the book is the boys' and girls' own talk, and in a format that simulates as faithfully as possible the impact of the handwriting, often as eloquent as voice itself. To reproduce some questionnaires was an obvious way to achieve this end. For the rest, direct transcription by typesetting typewriter—permitting odd spacing and other imitative effects—was a workable, if compromise, method with the advantage of having all the quotations from children in a vigorous bold-face letter easily distinguishable from the book-face style of the editorial matter.

As a frame of reference for reading that which is yet to come, you might recall that at the time these children were reporting back to us, there was much keening in the adult sector over "where did we go wrong?!" in raising our children. The hippies and the drugs, the Vietnam involvement, concern for the environment, violence and student protest were beginning sharply to disturb the national conscience and there had been already much doubt and questioning of our schools system, where all kinds of expensive gismos and "plant" couldn't hide the fact that fundamentally they had stood unchanged for forty years. The time was not quite yet for the moon walk, but the behavioral scientists were publishing some provocative new findings about children's mental development.†

†For a roundup of research and results in this field, see "A Child's Mind" (1970, New York, Doubleday & Company, Inc.) by Muriel Beadle. In relation to this book, her chapter on language is especially recommended.

List the things that bother you most about grown-ups.

a) They swear

b) They give you lickings

c) And when your grandmother comes up and she make you

List three things you will always remember to do around children when you grow up.

a) not to swear

b) not to tell them lies

c) not to smoke

List three things you promise you won't say or do to kids when you grow up.

a) not to swear

b) not to holler at them all the time

c) tell them to be polite

List three things which really trouble you about being a child.

a) you have to watch your sisters and brothers

b) you have to do dishes

c) you have to go to school

Any further comments? _____

Your Grade: Five   Your Age: 10

Above: What bothers this one reads plain and clear (the writing suggests a girl, but calligraphy proved to be an uncertain means for separating the sexes).

At right: The large capital-letter proclamation of sex across the bottom was marred by a broken M and the missing O in B Y, because he filled out his form with a ball-point pen that malfunctioned at precisely this juncture. Obviously the pen was made by some blackmailing adult who swats kids with spoons and won't let them drive even the cars they win in raffles.

...st the things that bother you most about grown-ups. (What bugs you?)

1) They boss you ~~around~~ around
2) You can't talk back to them.
3) They ~~~~ blackmail you

...st three things you will always remember to do around children when you
...ow up.

1) Not read the paper when they want to play
2) Play what they want to play

...st three things you promise you won't say or do to kids when you grow up.

1) Squat them with a spoon
2) Cuss

...st three things which really trouble you about being a child.

1) I can't drive ~~my~~ own car
2) I can't drink beer

...y further comments? I won it in a raffle

Your Grade: 5 Your Age: 10

ease return this sheet to: Stephen Greene, 120 Main St., Brattleboro, Vt. 05301

T A A B Y

19

Is what the children themselves say, then, of any matter? How seriously should they be heeded? Editor Greene kept warning: Don't over-interpret. Some of us kids [she said] do get lambasted and pushed around, but a lot of us have sense enough to know that stern treatment is sometimes due us.

Granted, but wherefore the "sadness that underlies many of the replies" that one of the teachers spoke of? Is there some one big thing, or an accumulation of **"stuf"** (grownups included), bothering kids in today's world?

For the moment, heed the words of a citizen of the metropolitan Midwest who, from the pinnacle of his or her 11 years, raps grownups' arthritic knuckles as follows . . .

They can't take a joke

. . . and furthermore . . .

Adults think all children are alike and develope at the same time.

Let [illegible] NAG them NOT [illegible]

List the things that bother you most about grown-ups.
a) _They always tell secrets and dont let us listen._
b) _They hardly ever pay any attention to us._
c) _They hardly ever do us favors._

List three things you will always remember to do around children when you grow up.
a) _Talk well manered around them._
b) _Act politely around them._
c) _Pay more attention to them._

List three things you promise you won't say or do to kids when you grow up.
a) _I wont slap them in the face._
b) _I wont brise them._
c) _I wont make them do all the work_

List three things that really trouble you about being a child.
a) _I can't go to flight school yet_
b) _No one will pay attention to my_
c) _car drawings. I want to get a job on a air force base._

Any further comments? _They talk about boys shouldnt take baths with girls. And they do it and say they can just because their married_

Your Town:_____ Your School:_____ Your Grade: _6_ Your Age: _11_
Are you a boy? _X_   Or Girl?___

Two forms from Sixth Grade show what a printing hobgoblin penciled hand-writing can be. The universal school writing medium is tricky and undependa-ble in reproduction. If any of the kids get to work in the graphic arts, this will bother them about grownups.

21

your own mistake

QUESTIONNAIRE FOR BOYS AND GIRLS

We know that there are a lot of things that we grownups do and say that bother or embarrass you. We'd like to know what these things are. Please answer these questions:

List the things that bother you most about grown-ups.

a) When something is wrong or you did something bad they always bug you. they never leave

b) they tell you not to do Swear or Something, And you turn And th

c) grown-ups don't understand our problems they JUST SAY ok, but when I was

List three things you will always remember to do around children when you grow up.

a) try to understand their ways of living in their time not own time

b) be very patient with them

c) be polite and Kind to them

List three things you promise you won't say or do to kids when you grow up.

a) I will try not to embarrass them IN front

b) of their friends or grown-ups

c) I won't tell them they Are wrong I will try to understand

List three things which really trouble you about being a child. And explai

a) grown-ups boss you Around they don't understand

b) having to learn on your own because parents

c) are to chicken to tell you the facts of life

Any further comments?

Your Town: ____ Your School: ____ Your Grade: 6 Your Age: 12

How do you spell grownups? The boys and girls have several variants. Three out of four dictionaries consulted spell it grownups *(one word, noun) and* grown *hyphen* up *(adjective). We have it both ways on the questionnaires. One of them is correct. Young friends, this is known as "hedging."*

CHAPTER III

WHAT BOTHERS THIRD GRADE MOST ABOUT GROWNUPS
Ages Eight and Nine

Any further comments? *I Know I made a mess.*

List the things that bother you most about grownups.

a)   I dont like it when grownups say "Hello Dear."
b)   I dont like it when grownups say "Look at the doll"
c)   Or "Whats you mame Honey?"

a)   When grandmothers come, and say, "My how you've grown.
b)   When mothers say "Pumkin poo!! "
c)   When fathers are so bossy.

Speaking are a Miss Eight and a Master Nine, their questionnaires chosen to lead off as a check on whether many of the children were influenced in their answers by the examples given on the instruction sheet. One of these felt strongly enough about our "my how you've grown" hint to give it top billing. Some others took our "they talk too much" suggestion as their chief complaint, asserting that . . .

They are always talking.
They take to much.
T h e y talk together toomuch a n d I get   bored

Following these three, a twice-telling anti-talker . . .

a)   They neve talk to you
b)   They are good to children
c)   They are talking all the time.

they don't pay much attention
they say to much
they talk to much

They dont let us talk.

When I am talking my Mother talks

However, even if we include one complaining that **"they snor too much"** the fraction of "influenced" questionnaires is tiny. A group of six didn't answer the lead question at all, and . . .

nothing
nothing
nothing

said it for one (who claimed, later, to be really troubled by . . .

skoolol
mother
father

in the order named). Then there are Tom, 8, who listed the things that bother him most about grownups as **They don't,** and Bonnie, 8, whose entire questionnaire reads:

nothing bothers me about gron-ups.
I will never be mean to a child
I will never smoke at children
nothing bugs me about being a child

Any further comments? **No**

At this point we've examined 19 out of 186 questionnaires sent back by Third Graders. Turning to the rest, we are informed that . . .

My mother and my father yell.

my mother and father holler at me

They bother me by yelling at me.
When they take to much.

They yell at you all the time.   They yell at me
They can say and do things that you can't.   and they hit me

drinking   yell
walking down the street drinking
do   not   hit

yell at us
beat us
they drive fast

When they hearer at me
When thaye make me eat
When thay call me names

They yell at you a lot.
They tease me alot.
They give me a lot of work.

They   yell   at   me.
They   make   me   go   to   bed   ealy.
They   make   me   do   the   dishes.

My   mother   yelling   at   me.
My   mother   making   me   work.
My   mother   doesn't   help   me   on   my   homework.

Thay   holler   at   us   and   geves   us   heck.
Thay   don't   let us   get   our   way   sometime.
Thay   don't   let us   Buy   some   candy

When   they   yell   at   you
When   the   doctor   gives   you   a   shot
When I can't sit in the front seat of the car

they yell at me.
they make me go to school.
My father won't play ball with. me

they yell at you
they beat you
they tell you to do to much.

They   holler   at you   if   your   late
if   your   sorry   they   still   get   mad
They   stop you   from going places

They   yell at   y o u.
They   dount   l e t y o u   stop   and   play
They   embarrassyou

They holler at you.
They hit you.
They don't let you go places.

They yell to much
They kill to much
They slam cupboards to much

when they yell at you.
when they strip you with belt.
when they punish you.

They   yell   to   much
They   make   fun   of   me
They   stop   me   from   going to the store

When she yell at me.
When she make me go to bed early.
Whenshemakeme gotothestoreallthetime.

They all Way yelling at   you
They make you do all   the work. an they dont.
They whip you so much.

They   yell   at   you   and   theypunishmet you
When you be bad   and when   you do
something   wourg.

thay yell and Brorer you to much.
thay argue at you and shake you.
and wont maim thar owne Bizneses

They   yell at littler children
They   punishment you for   nother
They   olway   hate people

No doubt above, it's grownups' *yelling* that bothers these young ones most. In the next batch to be quoted, the noise subsides to second place, as other behavior moves up to the top line.

Making you do the dishes   beating
yelling   yelling at me
Making you stay in the house   they punishment me

thay beat me
thay   yell at me
thay   argue with outher people

you keep get push a round
they yell at you for nothing
you you can n't even play

Thay anbarrass you in frontofyour friends
They yell at you when you get in trouble from the teacher
They make you clean your room allthe time

They get mad too much.   they hit me
They yell too much.   they yell at me
Grown-ups hit a lot.   my brother crabs

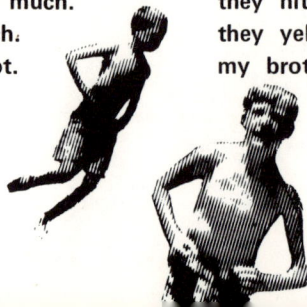

List the things that bother you most about grown-ups.

a) They yell at you all the time.

b) They can say and do things that you can't.

c) _____

List three things you will always remember to do around children when you grow up.

a) Talk to then.

b) Be kind to then

c) _____

List three things you promise you won't say or do to kids when you grow up.

a) never swer

b) _____

c) _____

List three things which really trouble you about being a child.

a) You don't have any power over grown-ups

b) _____

c) _____

List the things that bother you most about grown-ups.

a) They get mad.

b) They skold us.

c) They keep you moving.

List three things you will always remember to do around children when you grow up.

a) Put maches out of reach.

b) _____

c) _____

List three things you promise you won't say or do to kids when you grow up.

a) Get to bed at six.

b) Stop geting them crandy & soda pop.

c) _____

List three things which really trouble you about being a child.

a) Work troubles me

b) _____

c) _____

Any further comments? _____

_____ Your Grade: 3R gw   Your Age: 8

27

a) Most grown ups are strict.
b) They yell.
c) They wake you up in the night to give you medicine

List three things you will always remember to do around children when you grow up.

a) not to be strict.
b) not to yell.
c) not to wake people up and give them medicine

List three things you promise you won't say or do to kids when you grow up.

a) I will not say shut up or be quiet.
b) I will not put them to bed any later than 8:30
c)

List three things which really trouble you about being a child.

a) walking home
b) eating spinach.
c) eating broccoli.

Any further comments? I do not like to walk home because my sister, yells at me and hits me with her lunch box.

Your Grade: 3 Your Age: 8-9

List the things that bother you most about grown-ups.

a) I do not get to play.
b) My father and mother do not let me ride a horse.
c) My mother hits me to much!

List three things you will always remember to do around children when you grow up.

a) Take them to the fair.
b) Don't get mad all the time.
c) Don't be a sleeping beauty.

List three things you promise you won't say or do to kids when you grow up.

a) I will not say a bad word to a baby.
b) But usully it is ok.
c)

List three things which really trouble you about being a child.

a) I am to small and I want to
b) be biger than my sister!
c)

Any further comments? One more thing my sister is a stupid sister

Your Grade: 3 Your Age: 8-9

When the spak you.   Then   always hit me.
When they yell.   Then   shout   at me.
When they say go after milk.

Mother   and   Daddy   spanks   me.
And   Mother   and Daddy   hollers   at   me.

They   are   brosssy.   They   give us a spanking.
They   yell to   mach.   They   holler   at us.
They   give   me   it.   They   slap   us.

They   don't   take   you   out--
When they lose   something   they yell at you--
My babysitter   always   yell   at   us--

When my mother blames me for something I don't do
When they yell at me
    When they spank me.

When   I   get   scolded.   they   hit
When   my   father   yells.   they   holer   at you
When   my   uncle   hits me.   They   sceen   at you

theyer   to   bossy.
they   yell to   much.
they   do not   let   me   watch   my   shows *

They are bossy.
They yell at me.
They   don't   lit me watch T.V. **

Permit an editorial aside regarding the responses marked * and **
above. They are from the same school, same class. The thoughts and phrasing
are so alike that we wondered if this could be collusion between a couple of
kids sitting within peeking range of each other. We looked for, and found, a
miniscule percentage of similar instances. The evidence against much compar-
ing of notes by the children is what they say in other sections of the questionaires. Master or Miss *, above, in listing the things that really trouble him/her
about being a child, woefully remarked, **"I can't do things so good. I can't do
the things I want to do."** Classmate **, signing himself Tony, said, **"I get
blame on evrything."**

To continue, here is a third and smallest clutch listing grownups' "all
Way yelling at you," but now this is last in order of mention.

Smoking   They Showoff   a   lot.
Going out at night   They   hug   boys.
Hollering   They   scream.

My Parents hit me all the time.
My big brother   punches   me.
My Brother yells at me.

they blame thing on you.   cannot wtachT V
they are bossy.   c a n n o t e t a
they yell at us.   y e l l i n g

They send me to bed after supper
They usually tell meto eat allourdinner and supper
They say shout at you

When   my   Father takes hold of me
The Teacher gives us to hard of work
The Teacher hollers at me to much

My   uncle   spanks   me.
The teacher   gives   us   hard   work.
The teacher   holler   at me   to   much.

Before progressing further, let's nominate for the language the word
sceen ("They sceen at you"), coined by an anonymous Age Eight. It struck
us as an inspired misspelling, joyously combining *scream* and *keen* into a
term loaded with more and better decibels than either!

Why all this attention to *yelling, hollering, screaming,* and *shouting* at
children? Because it's the behavior pattern that one-third of our Third Graders point the finger at. Let's remember that eardrums are tender at this age;
even so, it might be expected that what bothers this age group most about
grownups is—punishment? Violence?

To find out, we scoured the questionnaires for words connoting action
with intent to make uncomfortable. The boys and girls themselves use: *hit,
spank* (expressed also as *lackins, lick), punish, push, beat, hurt, punch, slap,
shake, kick, kill,* and *strip* (as in "strip you with belt"). In the order listed,
hit and *spank* far outnumber all of the other words, but the lot together
comes to no more than the four noise words, of which *yell* is the decided favorite. The consensus is a shade in favor of grownups' bark over bite.

Some representative hit/spank opinion reads as follows:

Wenen theey   kit me.   They can hurt you.
They   smoke in the house.   They can kik you.
They   fight in the house.   They can puch you.

When they hit me   when ther y hit me.
When they sead me to bed   When they send me to bed.
When they leave me at home   when they get mad at me.

30

My Father when he comes
from B---------- He always.
hits me in the back.

grown-ups hit us when we are bad.
grown-ups do not let us saty up.
they have to which were T V.

they lick you
they hit you
they make you eat what's on your plate

I don't like my Mother to spank me .
I don't like to always work at home on Sunday and Saturday

They spank us
Every time they go away they get a baby siter.
They don't let us see a show we want to they turn it over.

Thay slap in the face.   They hit me.
Thay spank me.   They say things I can not undern stand.
O u r teacher is mean   They don't buy what I want.

When you ' re ashamed of something they tell other people.
Spankings and other things.
They are mean and cross sometimes.

They spank me in front of people
They're nicer to my Brother than they are to me
They go to nice places and leave me with
    a baby sitter

Four members of one class have little to say except . . .

Put you on punishment
    They punishment you
    They punishment me
    They punishment you for nother

. . . and, among our spankees, two more with added, allied grievances:

They make you sleep with your big sisters
They spank you to much.
They make you it all your dinner.

Spank me to much.
They make you sleep with a brother
Make me eat all my dinner

Meanness, teasing, name-calling, and "they pick on me" form a plaintive small chorus:

When they are mean
When she doesn't put me to work
When she doesn't comfort me when
I am sad

They pick on you   pick
They take stuf of mine.   call us names
they blame stuf on me.   push us

They are so mean
They shout at you sometimes.
They make us dry the dishes.

They pick on   me.

They   pick   on   you   all the time mostly your brothers

Call   us   names
Push   us
Picks   on   us

My   father   calls   me   fatty.
When they kid you every time   it bothers me.
When you get punished.
They scold you over a little thing.

They get mad.
They skold us.
They keep you moving.

to   stop   teasing   me   When they tease me.
stop   calling   me   names   When they boss me around.
stop   being   cross   to   me   When I have to work.

They   treat me unfairly
They   always say no
They   always hit me.

That they nag you.   THEY THINK you are a BABY
We half to work.   THEY are Mean
They never play with me.   We can't chew paper or gum

they nag you
some People don't answer your questions
Some kids never see much of their parents

We tried to be eagle-eyed for comments on grownups' smoking and tippling. Third Grade didn't have much to say; only three (one quoted earlier) give first place to these adult addictions. From a boy, nine: **They smoke and the smoke gets in my eyes,** followed by **they drink,** and then, what's more, **they open gifts before Christmas!**

They are smoking all the time, they drink a lot, and **they spank to much** agrees another nine-year-old, sex not revealed, who elaborates these thoughts with: **Its always grown-up time.**

There is the early-bedtime syndrome—of which more in a later chapter— and a body of opinion about food and force-feeding. See above, and. . .

They burn my favorite food sometimes.

Then grown -ups eat.
The grown- ups talk a otl.
Grown -ups malk you eat.

grownups plays trick on me.
grownups make me eat foot.

I don't like beans my mom makes me eat **them**

Ma makes me eat gulosh

They always say you better not eat candyoryou'll get a cavity.

"I'm the baby of the family and my parents almost try to spoil me," adds this young miss, age nine, and she returns to the food theme again, concluding her questionnaire with **I have to eat everything on my plate.**

Overwhelming to one Age Eight struggling to be articulate are these dismal conditions: **Grow-up are to bag. Grow-up are to bag and bocy. Grow-up are to an grownups.** Another one puts it this way. . .

They think they are bbig.
they think they can Boeys you around.
they think they can yous you like a Dog

A boy and a girl pair up as follows on the "boss us around" complaint:

Thier bossy.	**They are bossy.**
They blame us for things we don't do.	**They make us do the dishes.**
They make us go to bed early.	**They don't have time to play.**

We find these sentiments, too, in reverse phrasing, as **when they tell you to do something** and **you always have to do what they say.**

Childrens' unhappiness, disappointment, and general ruefulness over being "left out of things" get such notices from Third Grade as . . .

there always hideing thing from use.
going places with out me.
not lating me go places
When my parents go out to dinner
they hardly ever take me

They can spack me
The can make me do a lot of work
They go places without me

All together, now, boys and girls! . . .

a dot like the teacher to make me sit in my sait

my sister is beauti f e e l my little sister bugs me

They say no when I want them to say yes

List the things that bother you most about grown-ups.
a) When they blame something on you.
b) They push you around.
c) They put me to bed early.

List three things you will always remember to do around children when you grow up.
a) I will help them with their work.
b) I will help them read.
c) I will help them cross the road

List three things you promise you won't say or do to kids when you grow up.
a) I will never spank them.
b) I will never punish them.
c) I will never hit them with a stick.

List three things which really trouble you about being a child.
a) I have to do the dishes every night.
b) I never can play the piano.
c) I never can laugh in the car.

Any further comments?

Your School: _____ Your Grade: 3 Grade Your Age: 8

34

They make you do work.
They have more fun than we do.
They can be a teacher and we can't
They dom't play with me
When they mak the thing I don't like.
When people are in a great herry on Sat.
When people kill animals.

They mack you rush   They think they so big
They mack you work.   Something they are good.
They mack you talk decent.   Something they good.

fighting with my sister and brother
W h e r e h a v e y o u b e e n B r o t h e r
fighting with my sisters.

List the things that bother you most about grown-ups.

a) _Smoking_

b) _Going out at night_

c) _Hollering_

List three things you will always remember to do around children when you grow up.

a) _Take care of Them,_

b) _Help them_

c) _Make them happy_

List three things you promise you won't say or do to kids when you grow up.

a) _Hunt them_

b) _Dont make them do bad things._

c) _Fight_

List three things that really trouble you about being a child.

a) _Can't go places_

b) _Going to school_

c) _Trying to make a friend (It is hard)_

Any further comments? _____

_____

_____

_____

Are you a boy? _yes_   Your Grade: _3_ Your Age: _9_
                              Or Girl? ____

35

T h e r e b i g g e r t h a m m e
T h e y a r e t o s t r i c t.
t h e y d o n o t g i v e m e e n o u g ht m o n e y
They bother me by fighting.
They make me wach the dishes.
They make me go to bed
Grown-upare smrtter. And they aresmrtter then us.
They are bigger then us.
Grown ups boss us around.
They make you do thing you do
not want to.They cook thing you do
not want to eat
They always said do this so that
They always are nice to my brother and sister
My Mothers is m a d at us all the time
Speak about my business.   tell people what do
They aren't fair.   nicer to my brother
Does not like fast music.   sometimes she is nad

you can not talk back at them
they love my brother and sister but not me.
they say to do everthing.
            they tell the people everthing.
                  they talk when you are talking.
Git mad.   We are never able to stay
Go a way and leave me home   with the grown-ups when
                                          they are talking.

Wistfully, from a questionnaire previously quoted: **They want me to go away.** "When they blame something on you" sounds in a number of the questionnaires, as in this one from a girl midway between eight and nine:

When they punish me for something I didn't do
When they won't let me go on the road
When they won't let me talk to them

Here are nine- and eight-year-olds on the subject of a kind of behavior that would send anybody up a wall:

The questions they ask   the question they usually ask you
were have you ben   they pick on you
do so many jobs

. . . and one, he or she not specified, who says it with a bill of particulars:

List the things that bother you most about grown-ups.

a) *when I am doing a singing song I get cerected*
b) *and when Im eating I can be mad I get cerected*
c) *then when I interrupting I get cereted.*

Nor does this one leave it at that. The questionnaire concludes . . .

List three things which really trouble you about being a child.

a) *I am trying like my Ramley.*
b) *and I am allways yolld at!*
c) *and I am allways cerected,*

Any further comments? *no*

From out West, pioneer land of the freeway, some comment on grown-ups' driving:

they   know   how   to   drive.
they   go   out.
they   have   money

When   thay   go   out.
thay   get   mad   to   much.
thay   drive   to   fast.

there nicer to my little sister.
they arnt   fair   in   games.
they   always   show   off   their   good   driveing.

They   stay   out   to   long
my   Dad   drive   to   fast

They drive to fast.
They always love my sister.
They dot let   met me   to the park

Only a few Third Graders left to quote. One who says that the trouble with being a child **"is being a 9 year old girl"** states that grownups bother her because . . .

they were lipstick. they go to moves. they dive in cars.

Still more from the distaff side:

when my brothers & sister bother me at homework
when my parents don't let me climb trees
when sometimes my mother won't let me buy things.

They do not hurt me.
Sometime they do hurt me?
They play.

They usually say "NO."
They are not fair.
They are always
on your brothers Side.

When they worry.
When they are telling secrets about you.
And when they are mad at you.

A boy, 8½, considering himself underprivileged because **I can not take out girls,** lists these two strikes on grownups:

**They don't give you enouth allowonce
They fight all the time**

There speaks a potential big spender but, good friend, beware! In our day there was a type of girl known as a "gold digger," and one of these can shrink to nothing any amount of "allowonce" you'll ever be given, or earn. Meanwhile, *Any further comments?* . . .

It is in the higher grades that the boys and girls put to best use this portion of their questionnaires. Nevertheless, 40 percent of our Third Grade responders put something in, even if only a **no, not now, nothing,** or **I can't think of anything more to say.** Some of these final remarks bear on what the child has already said, and should not be quoted out of context. But here are some that can:

I wish my mother would let me ride my blind pony Flika more

I would like to be let to mow a lawn. I like girls and they never like me.

I H a t e Bo y ' s ! but I love my dad

I want to get out fo hear and i hate girl

I love my mom and dad but they nearly drive me out of my head sometimes.

I don't know why big people have to boss us around like toys! Why can't we boss them around for once?

I have to walk even if its below 0.

I't bothers me when grownups don't let me go out side.

When my mother makes me practice

Yes.   I don't have any sister. I have to many brothers (5) of them, They tease me to much and I get mad.

One Age Eight was prompted to write: **I thing your silly.** But he erased it. Thanks, son; one of our welts is assuaged.

e know that there are a lot of things that we grownups do and say that
other or embarrass you. We'd like to know what these things are. Please
nswer these questions:

ist the things that bother you most about grown-ups.

) You never get any rest they are always telling you to do something.

) When ever I'm going to go outsi she make me practice.

) They are past sixty and so want something or they say their too busy.

ist three things you will always remember to do around children when you
row up.

) To be kind.

) To say the right words.

) Do the right thing.

ist three things you promise you won't say or do to kids when you grow up.

) I wont spank any kids, but my own.

) I won't say things that they will cry.

) I wont let the play with plastic bags for the could suffocate

ist three things which really trouble you about being a child.

) People always baby me.

) Peope accuse me of things I didnt do

) People always tell my secrets.

y further comments? I think this is the silliest thing
I've ever head of. Why do you ask such
nasy questions?

Your Grade: 4 Your Age: 9

The works—from one of our severest critics.

39

1. They dislike Negroes, they think there big shots, they smoke

2. pay attention to them, set a good example, not spoil my children

3. swear, cuss, and smoke. (if I do)

4. you can't go to things your older brothers and sisters go to. I get to much allowance. My father is almost never home he's always on buisness trips.

In one classroom the teacher seems to have copied our questions on the chalk-board, for the children wrote their answers in the form shown here. We have followed their numbering as a means of identifying the questions in the text, using, however, the Arabic, or Old Math, numerals in preference to the Roman, or Ancient Math, notation.

I. When they say that they will do something for me but they forget.

II. Play games, go out with other boys (Definatly not girls) and do other stuff.

III. Say that I do not like there personallity.

IV. Mostly everybody hates me, they like other people better than me, and they get me out in all the games that I play with them.

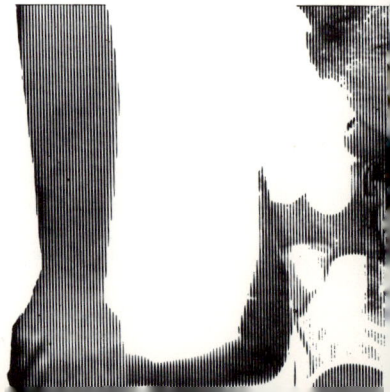

CHAPTER IV

WHAT BOTHERS FOURTH GRADE MOST ABOUT GROWNUPS

Ages Nine and Ten

b) *Don't act like Donald Duck for kids over 7.*

Your Grade: 4 Your Age: 9 3/4

THE EXHIBIT above appears in answer to our Question 2: *List three things you will always remember to do around children when you grow up.* There is no clue to whether a boy or girl is speaking. Because he or she starts off listing some things that bother Fourth Graders more than they did our Third Grade friends, here is the rest of the questionnaire:

1.a) **They don't let you spend money.**
  b) **They don't take you where you want to go.**
  c) **They don't let you do things.**
2.a) **Not to scold in front of other people.**
  b) **Don't act like Donald Duck for kids over 7.**
  c) **Let them watch TV.**
3.a) **Don't scold very much.**
4.a) **Your parents.**

Let's not assume (because he/she gives it top billing) that this young one believes that money is everything. Let's just take it that here is awareness of money as well as a complaint lodged against grownups' restrictiveness. Fourth Grade *vs.* Third Grade also evinces more interest in clothes and autos.

The reference to Donald Duck beautifully ticks off the adult posture of noisy omnipotence. Speaking of noise, we can set our hearing aids back to

normal, because in Fourth Grade objections to grownups' yelling and hollering abate by half, although the children's vocabulary of sound is just as vigorous. **"They almost always shaught at me,"** says one (we assume he/she means
"shout," not "shoot").

In the same ratio there is a decline in comment on violent punishment—
indicating an increase in the toughness of young hides? But no new words for
hit and *spank;* these two serve Fourth Grade admirably.

As a partial picture of the action in Fourth Grade over Third Grade,
here is a sort of box score. As our quantities are not large, the "ups" and
"downs" are in terms of the percentage of response on a particular matter in
relation to the number of kids in each grade who answered Question 1. When
capital letters are used, it is to emphasize a markedly noticeable trend.

Boss us around	up
Don't let us have or do what we want	UP
Make us do work	slightly up
Make us do extra work	definitely up
Restrict our going and coming	UP
Are always, or sometimes, interfering	UP
Make us go to school, do homework	down
Make us eat what we don't want, clean our plates	down
Objection to grownups' drinking, smoking, swearing	UP
Control or denial of the TV	DOWN
They embarrass us	up a notch
Have no time for us, won't listen to us	UP
Get mad over little or nothing	up
Keep their secrets and tell ours	UP
Hit, spank, punish	DOWN
Yell, holler, scream	DOWN
Talk too much	UP
—especially on the telephone	*way* up

What bothers Fourth Grade most about grownups, quantitatively speaking, remains in Editor Greene's big, general classification which she labeled:
Bossiness, Punishment, Rules.

As a preliminary to enjoying what the kids themselves say about things,
the Senior Editor interjects that he was suddenly reminded in this batch of
questionnaires of an event in the Human Condition, Fourth Grade Division,
that he hadn't thought of in years. If he remembers correctly, a significant
milestone of childhood was the birthday when one moved up from a one-digit
to a two-digit age. The attitude is: I'm 10 now, and grownups ought to know
at a glance that I'm one of Them. Naturally, grownups remain obtuse on this

point (one finds out) but the least they can do is realize that *10-years-old* is the point of no return, ever, to *infancy*. Grownups should behave accordingly. Instead, **they baby us, treat you like babies, call you baby names.** Well, not all, but enough do to flavor our Fourth Grade responses with a dash of cynicism, a pinch more of exasperation, compared to Third Grade. They, grownups, **get too nervas.** From a 10-year-old boy's point of view, why should **My Mother get scared when you go horses bake ride**? To a brand-new Master or Miss Age 10, isn't it a kind of ultimate in babying when **They say I can't blow my nose and I can?**†

  They don't let you do things is the way that almost-10, the 9¾-year-old Donald Duck fan, puts it (page 41). His or her resolve not to scold **in front of other people** is something to bear in mind, too, because at this age more boys and girls than formerly are beginning to carp in that vein.

  Unless otherwise indicated, all quotations following are in response to Question 1. Since the matter of grownups **talk too much** looms fairly large in the Fourth Grade consciousness, we present initially two forms in reproduction (on pages immediately following) and . . .

> **They talk to much.**
> **They are to bossy.**
> **Most don't have manners.**
>
> **They talk to much.**
> **They go places to much.**
> ~~and~~ **They kiss you.**
>
> **They talk to much**
> **They don't let you drink wine or coffee until your 21 (or 1₄**
>
> **They take to much.**
> **They are sometimes grouchy.**
> **That they shout to much.**
>
> **They take to long on the telephone.**
> **They work to hard.**
> **They get to drive.**
>
> **They talk a lot after supper**
> **They want you to do too many things**
> **They won't let you do what you want to do**

(For coffee)

†In all grades is a very small percentage of boys and girls of an age over the norm for the group, held back because of performance or perhaps for no more reason than that their birthdays didn't mesh with the placement machinery of the school system in authority. Thus, in counting the Fourth Grade questionnaires to see if children of age 10 do outnumber the nine-year-olds (they do) we included these older ones of 11 and 12. A tally of questionnaires sounding the "being babied" note and critical of grownups' overprotectiveness again gives the edge to the 10-and-over ages, among whom the boys seem rather more irked than the girls.

List the things that bother you most about grown-ups.

a) _talk and talk on and on_

b) _They never let me go any place over night_

c) _never let me watch t.v._

List three things you will always remember to do around children when you grow up.

a) _Not talk to a person on and on_

b) _get mad_

c) _help them_

List three things you promise you won't say or do to kids when you grow up.

a) _just leave me alone!_

b) _shut up!_

c) _go to bed_

List three things which really trouble you about being a child. _with every_

a) _I would—let my sister get away_

b) _let my brother hit me_

c) _let sister be such bross_

Any further comments? _make my sister clean her bedroom. Why does my sister who is older get away with every thing_

Your Grade: _4_   Your Age: _9½_

Most mothers have phones, they will talk
What bothers me is that when they to much on it
whip you, and you don't cry, they whip you more. (some of THEM)

My parnets talk to mush on the telephone
My parnets aloys are gone
My mother alloys has a fr end or two over

. . . and, says this one later on: I do not get to talk on the telephone

ist the things that bother you most about grown-ups.

a) We you get ready to talk they start to talk

b) To clean the house

c) And get up in the morning

ist three things you will always remember to do around children when you row up.

a) Be kind to them when they asked you something

b) And do not sent them out doors when it is cold

c) Teach them to say the righ words

ist three things you promise you won't say or do to kids when you grow up.

a) Do not put them out side when it is raining out

b) And do not hit them for what other kids do

c) When the child does not eat all his food do not make him or her.

ist three things which really trouble you about being a child.

a) They get in bed with you and push you out

b) When you get a drink they want it

c) When you have lipstick they eat it

ny further comments? _____

_____

_____

_____

Grade: 4 Your Age: 11

They talk alot on the telephone
They hesitate about buying things
They hesitate about letting you ride your bike down the road
Eveything worrys them.
They never have time to talk to you.
They are always talking on the phone.

(Even so, **I think grown-ups are very nice** adds this Age 9.)

45

Their appetite
They never want to play
They talk for a long time

Abruptly a Miss Age 10, writing so fast that it looks as though her mind couldn't keep up with her pencil, states at the top of her questionnaire:

My mother talks to much about.

And what, children, is a grownup likely to talk about? . . .

They talk to much. Theytalk about you

They talk too much about me.

When they talk about me.
When they treat you like babies.
When they talk aboutthethings that I do.

they sometimes talk about your personal things
sometimes they yell at you when
                                         when you have a friend over

. . . and some grownups do this kind of talking where?

My dad talks about me in front of people
Hes always talking about me
My baby brother and my dad

They always say your so pretty or how you've grown.
They talk about me in front of people

They say were darlings.
They yell at you in public.

When they yell at you in front of company.

They spank you in front of people.

When they embarrass me infront of my friends or relitives.

A nine-year-old quoted above winds up with I like it to sometimes be quiet and its almost always not. I don't like arguments and fights. Agreeing with her, a boy, same age, proclaims . . .

They are always argueing
They are always blaming me without letting me explain.
They always tell other people what I do.

When they tell other grownups what youve been punished for.
When they have family arguments once in a long while.
When they go out and don't come back till very late.

. . . and this Miss Age 10 is irked enough to comment further: When parents

swear at you rightin frontof your friends.

They say embarrassing things about you (Age 10), and **When they lecture you** reports a nine-year-old, one of a few individuals who register embarrassment also as **They stare at you,** specifically in this case as **When a storekeeper watches everything you do (In other words he hawk-eys you).**

As an end to all the talk about talking and in-front-of-people embarrassment, we reproduce the questionnaire below. And now the editor is embarrassed. He said that Fourth Grade produced no new words for *hit* and *spank*. He stands corrected by a boy or girl of 10, giving us **wip,** which has a fine cutting edge to it. Imagine being **wip**ped with, say, a cat-o'-nine-tails.

It would be pleasant to enjoy at length the ebullient company in Fourth Grade, but time, space, and Fifth and Sixth grades press us. The remainder of this chapter presents a gaggle of questionnaires sounding various notes, chosen

---

List the things that bother you most about grown-ups.

a) _Well they talk to much on the phone._

b) _Well my mother only let's my brother go and try run_

c) _And they get to wip us children._

List three things you will always remember to do around children when you grow up.

a) _Well if is a baby Do not wip it hard._

b) _In front of people, do not look at it._

c) _And Do not wip a child in front of people._

List three things you promise you won't say or do to kids when you grow up.

a) _I well not set on the telephone and talk._

b) _And if they want something I well get it for_

c) _If it needs help with it work, I well help_

List three things which really trouble you about being a child.

a) _Well, I can not go to the story by myself._

b) _My brother gets to do more thing than_

c) _And I do not to more the lawn_

Any further comments?_____

_____

_____

_____

Your Grade: _4_ Your Age: _10_

47

List the things that bother you most about grown-ups.

a) When they give you heck in public.

b) They go to the Leigion and I can't go.

c) They can spank you but you can spank them.

List three things you will always remember to do around children when you grow up.

a) Be nice to them.

b) Take them to the drive-in every Saturday.

c) Teach them safety rules so they won't get hurt.

List three things you promise you won't say or do to kids when you grow up.

a) I won't spank them much.

b) I won't swear at them.

c) I won't tell them to, "get lost"

List three things which really trouble you about being a child.

a) Teachers give you lots of Home work

b) You get spanked even if you didn't do it.

c) Grown-ups can do things I can't.

Any further comments? No

Your Grade: fourth Gr. Your Age: 9

---

with more concern for individuality expressed than for what may be revealed about the children's "bothers." It bothers *us* that we may slight a trend in so doing; for example, the complaint that grownups **never play with us.** Enough of it appears to remind us clearly that at this level one of the good things to share with children is simply—play. But the young ones mix it all up with other things, and their rue loses out to their roar.

Still in response to Question 1 . . .

"They Can, We Can't; They Get, They Do, We Don't"

When they say you cant go somewhere
When they say you cant go skidooing
And when you have to buy the gas

When they get mad at you
Making you play outside when it is cold.

List the things that bother you most about grown-ups. (What bugs you?)

a) They don't let you go anyplace.

b) They worried about my grades too much.

c) They also say how much now have grown.

List three things you will always remember to do around children when you grow up.

a) Always play with them.

b) Give them candy, but not too much.

c) Travel alot with them.

List three things you promise you won't say or do to kids when you grow up.

a) Boss them around.

b) I'll let them wear shorts and short dresses.

c) I'll let them swim and have parties any time when I feel like it.

List three things which really trouble you about being a child.

a) Going to school.

b) Playing baseball.

c) Growing up.

Any further comments? _____

Grade: 4 Your Age: 9

They get to drive a car. They get to have pizzas.
They always drink pop when they want it.

Any further comments? I think grown-ups get thier way enough.

They get things I like, like ice cream.
They get to go out to dinner a lot.
They make me sit in a lady-like position.

They get mad at you to easy.
They make me eat things you don't like.
They get to do what ever they want.

They get mad with a child over a little thing!

They always get mad.
Parents are always say, "Don't do this and that."
Also they're always saying NO!

49

They get mad at you for things they do themselves.

Sometimes they get the wrong impression and blame you for
Some, pamper you to much. something you didn't do.

When their mad we're scared.

"They Won't Let; They Make Me"

Grown - ups make there kids mind them.

When my mother puts false eyelashes on.

When my mother makes me go to bed.

They make yow go to bed when your not
tired They make you eat when you are not
hungry They never listen to childrenens idies

List the things that bother you most about grown-ups.

a) They tell you to do something and then get mad at you for doing it.

b) _____

c) _____

List three things you will always remember to do around children when you grow up.

a) Make them obey.

b) Dont let them go out without.

c) Watch them if their little.

List three things you promise you won't say or do to kids when you grow up.

a) I won't say naughty words to them.

b) I won't spank them if they do something wrong when their sick.

c) I won't let one child be treated very nice. And the other one terrible.

List three things which really trouble you about being a child.

a) Being the youngest.

b) Getting hand-me-downs.

c) _____

Any further comments? Yes I hope it will change.

_____

_____

_____

Your Grade: 4 Your Age: 10

My brother won't let my go anywhere.   Say Go to bed early
My mom makes me do the dishes.   spank you
My dad makes me wash the car.   They help you dress

When they wake me up early
When they make me go to bed early
When they give me no *(sic)* work to do

My brother sits on me to much
My brother won't let me use his 2 2 rifle
They make me do all the work

They boss me around.
They look down toward us.
I feel that I am not trusted.

List the things that bother you most about grown-ups.

a) _when the boys kick the ball_

b) _when the teacher gives me hell_

c) _when my father gives me hell_

List three things you will always remember to do around children when you grow up.

a) _Not to give them hell too much_

b) _not to holler at them so they want cry_

c) _Not to be mean to them_

List three things you promise you won't say or do to kids when you grow up.

a) _Not to push them down in a mean way_

b) _Not to be mean to them_

c) _Not to say mean words_

List three things which really trouble you about being a child.

a) _I wish when I am grown up I don't do what the boys do_

b) _I wish when I am grown up I hope I will be nice_

c) _I wish when I am grown I hope I like children_

Any further comments?_____

_____

_____

Your Grade: __4__   Your Age: __10__

List the things that bother you most about grown-ups.

a) They always step on your toes.

b) There always going somewhere.

o c) The afraid of snakes.

List three things you will always remember to do around children when you grow up.

a) Act just right.

b) Do things you should

c) look good.

List three things you promise you won't say or do to kids when you grow up.

a) I wont spank them.

b) I wont let them eat the thing that phd

c) I will treat them nice.

List three things which really trouble you about being a child.

a) you don't have a Baby of your own,

b) _____

c) _____

Any further comments? _____

_____

_____

Your Grade: 4   Your Age: 9

When I finish one job my mother tells me to do another.
I always have to wash my hands.

They never let you do things on your own
I think mothers are to do the work and they always make us.
We are supposed to do what our parents do and I know that sometimes
   they don't do the right things

Any further comments?   the other day I made a hole in the wall and I
have told my mother but not my father the reason for this is I know
what he will do.

"Smoke, Drink, Say Bad Things"

They Smoke
They   ride   motorcycles

List the things that bother you most about grown-ups. (What bugs you?)

a) *When they fight,*
b) *When they get mad at you*
c) *When they spank you*

List three things you will always remember to do around children when you grow up.

a) *The things you want them to do*
b) *Teach them to do things*
c) *Take them to school*

List three things you promise you won't say or do to kids when you grow up.

a) *Say I hate them*
b) *Spank them*
c) *Kill them*

List three things which really trouble you about being a child.

a) *Shots*
b) *Getting sick*
c) *Getting hurt*

Any further comments? *Why didn't you have us put our names on this sheet?*

Your Grade: *4* Your Age: *10*

They smoke and cough
They drink and get drunk
They sware and use bad language

When mom or dad say cuss words.
When dad drinks beer.
When people smoke cigrets.

They give you too much work.
They tell us not to do something and then they do it
They say swears.

They smoke and drink.
They think their the complete boss.
They won't let with your things.†

†Corrected in Question 4.a) to: "They take some of your things."

53

He drinks too much

They are too big

They go to dances

They sit too long on the stool

There apatite

They smoke

Grownups are sometimes too nosy. Why can't we keep secrets?
I hate to hear grown-ups swear. (or any one)

People who don't go to Church because they don't believe in God.

smoke

swear

drive to fast

They smoke to much.

They drink to much.

They talk to much.

When mom or dad say cuss words.

When dad drinks wiskey, beer, or skotch.

When dad drives to fast.

They said bad wrods.

They give us a spake.

The teacher she is sometime she is cross at me.

They say swears.

Their unfair about things.

They never consult us on things there going to buy.

"Thae bug me in more than one way"

Thae think thar big and sometime get it wrong.

Thae like you and then thae do not.

They usually punish first, ask later.

when my father goes somewhere like The P----- I-- (a moter lodge
that has a bar or to a movie he hardly ever takes me.

They Pull the blanket off of y o u a t m o r n i n g.

They hit you at night.

You get home late and you c a n n o t h a v e s u p p e r.

I hate when they fight and kill each other   hit.

How my father doesn't like jazz music.

My they send there good cars away for.

My we don't get a ride to school on a horse.

W hen they are in a hurry they rush you.

W hen   they play with there false theeth

When your sister starts a fight and your mother and farther blame you.

when you have to pick up toys that somebody els does.

when the teacher gets mad at you

They bother me when they speak other language's

when my dad tickles me
when he pretens to throw me over a cliff
when we go swimming my dad pushes me in when I'm not looking

They always now that I have not made my bed when I'm ready
to play.
     Their to smart for me.

Ladys put on too much make-up and take to long in the bath room.
Teathers give you home work. And then the parnets make you do it.
They baby you.

They never play with you when you want them to.
They buy you baby toy's.
They never let you go places.

When you ask a grown-up somming and he doesn't answer.
They push you around and think your nothing.
They always make you do somming you don't want to do.

Their temper
Not spending enough time with you

I try to make someone happy and somebody gets angry at me.
Sometimes the say 'no' and I don't think they have a good reason to
     say no.

grown-ups don't tell me things I want to know
grown—ups think I'm to small to do things that I can do
grown—ups won't let me say anything

They try to show off.
They go right on when there is a train stop.
They drive to fast.

. . . and on and on and on. Remember, however, that we grownups in-
vited them to talk.

Amid the cloudburst of Fourth Grade conversation, a clear statement of
being bothered most because of . . .

The facts of life.
How the world is growing.
What the people are doing now days.

. . . from an Age 10 boy or girl. We, too—and glad to have you aboard. We can
assure you that the troubles you list in Question 4 will pass away. They are:

Not being the right age to drive.
Not being good in subtects.
Not being the age can go places.

List the things that bother you most about grown-ups.

a) How will I know where to pay my bills?
b) What job will I take when I grow up?
c) Why do old people gosup more than young ones?

List three things you will always remember to do around children when you grow up.

a) I will be nice and won't stare at children.
b) I will not poke fun at any children.
c) And, I will be courteis.

List three things you promise you won't say or do to kids when you grow up.

a) I won't push them,
b) Nor curse them,
c) Or even punish other persons children.

List three things which really trouble you about being a child.

a) I wish I was big enough to do grownup things for
b) my mother when she is very sick.

List the things that bother you most about grown-ups.

a) They have lots of money.
b) They're so bossy.
c) They are always talking about bills.

List three things you will always remember to do around children when you grow up.

a) Be carful and watch then carfuly.
b) I won't just let them go.
c) I won't let them say in street.

List three things you promise you won't say or do to kids when you grow up.

a) I won't beat them up.
b) I won't hallar at them.
c) I won't shove them.

List three things which really trouble you about being a child.

a) Everyone tell you about girlbres.
b) If him lots of girl the r-l.
c) If her you like a girl.

Any further comments? Yes I wonder if it would be nsyd to be merried.

The two questionnaires, page opposite, present a range of concern over money—on top, worry; at bottom, envy. In between there are such as . . .

I like money and they don't give me much.

Sometimes they don't even let you buy 1¢ toys.

They worry too much about money.

When they are out of money they get grouchy.

. . . plus a murmur of annoyance over not enough allowance, and delays in paying same. And for one Fourth Grader it's not only money, but women. Read again the lower form, opposite.

What the kids have to say about boy-girl relationships isn't voluminous, but we introduce it at this level because of an incident. A summer-jobbing handygirl in the office helped reorganize the questionnaires after a bout of work had mixed them all up. One day she said, "The Fourth Graders say more about marriage." With obeisance to the feminine eye, here is what bothers and/or intrigues Fourth Grade about grown-up behavior oriented on male-female repulsion and attraction. Or about their own growing-up to it . . .

1.a) **they always say things about your girl-friend**
   b) **if you do something wrong, something little, they get real angry**

In Questions 2 and 3, no comment. From Question 4:

You can't do what grow - up do.
You can't stay up long at night.
You can't go on dates.

We can not drink.
You can not go on dates.

We get pushed around.
They make us do all the work.
They won't let us date until we are something like 15, 16, 17, or 18.

I can not drive a car
You can not go on dates

So I would know how to do things in the kitchen
So I would be a good wife

I have to wait to get married
You can't get married.

you can not do things alone.
you can not go sliding by yourself
you can not go on dates as you want to do.

The lightface type shows where this Age Nine worked over his or her comment with an eraser. Finally, from Question 5 . . .

Any further comments?   I thing I can not do the things I do wrong, and the thinges I can't do to get my self in troble. I should be good to my wife when I get married.

Boys always get to do the good things, like go fishing and play baseball. I've got a boyfriend and he won't pay any attention to me.

I hope I grow up fast and then I won't be left out of things. I want to be a framer. Then I could go on dates

I like all girls most boy's eiven yow. I don't like the boy's that bother me about my look's.

You   don't have a Baby of your own.

Below is a questionnaire in a thousand, literally! It is the only one of all of them that was filled out on the typewriter.

List the things that bother you most about grown-ups.
a)_____ They talk to much
_____
b)_____
c)_____

List three things you will always remember to do around children when you
grow up.
a)_____ I will nowevrr spit arond childern
_____
b)_____ I 2wwant nowever be impolite to chiXXdern
_____
c)_____ I will ever be mad to cHlden
_____

List three things you promise you won't say or do to kids when you grow up.
a)_____ I won;'t swear
_____
b)_____ I won't be impolite
_____
c)_____

List three things which really trouble you about being a child.
a)_____ _____ notong
_____
b)_____
c)_____

Any further comments?_____
_____
_____
_____
                                        4
_____Your Grade:____Your Age:10

CHAPTER V

WHAT BOTHERS FIFTH GRADE MOST ABOUT GROWNUPS

Ages Ten and Eleven

Any further comments? *Yes, I think kids should be the bosses.*

SOME YEARS AGO one of us sat in a Sunday School classroom wondering how to get the attention of seventeen chattering Fifth Graders who seemed chiefly interested in being somewhere else. Ah, let us try roll call as an opening gambit. But the beauty queen of the class—a miniature blonde Miss America of Christian upbringing—beat teacher to it. Into the quiet ensuing as he rose to his feet, she dropped this bomb: "I DON'T BELIEVE IN GOD!"

We'll all be off to a good start with Fifth Grade if we remember that these boys and girls are closer to puberty than they are to the playpen, and not go into shock when some of them indulge in capital-I iconoclasm and gleeful, sometimes heartfelt, image-breaking at grownups' expense. Grownups needing it can take some comfort in recalling that, at these ages, their little angels sometimes take cover by backsliding into that infancy they otherwise profess to scorn.†

One of the Fifth Grade questionnaires demonstrates this gamut in reverse (in handwriting, incidentally, that should bring delight to a teacher somewhere in our great land). The answer to Question 1 is typical of Third Grade. It reads . . .

1.a) **Being bossed around.**
  b) **Being yelled at.**

†Legally, all persons are infants until 21. Don't tell the boys and girls, or even more will insist that "kids should be the bosses."

59

In subsequent responses, it is as though the child were growing before your eyes in a time-lapse movie sequence . . .

2.a) **Have good manners.**
  b) **Be poliet.**

3.a) **Discuss money.**
  b) **Talk about outrageous subjects.**

4.a) **Having to do unfavorite things.**

Any further comments?　　　**Some parents are so particular and showoffish that I can't stand it.**

Hail, those "unfavorite" things! And that diplomatic "some" parents that he/she uses in berating a grown-up posture that gravels Fifth Grade more than its juniors. Another sagacious Age 10, yearning toward the adult freedoms symbolized by cars, trucks, late hours, and **big fat wallets,** is on guard as follows against the vengeance that begins at home . . .

Any further comments?　　　**yes. If my mother or father gets ahold of this　There going to tan my hide.**

As an example of grown-up diplomacy, we refrain from quoting more.

The Fifth Grade supplies 30 percent of all the questionnaires, exceeding Third and Fourth grades by more than a hundred each. Perhaps for this reason alone Fifth Graders give the impression of being more voluble and loquacious, but there must be a broadening of horizons as well, because the lower grades are less productive of questionnaires as jam-packed and wide-ranging as the one shown on the next page. Only 10 in Fifth Grade left Question 1 blank.

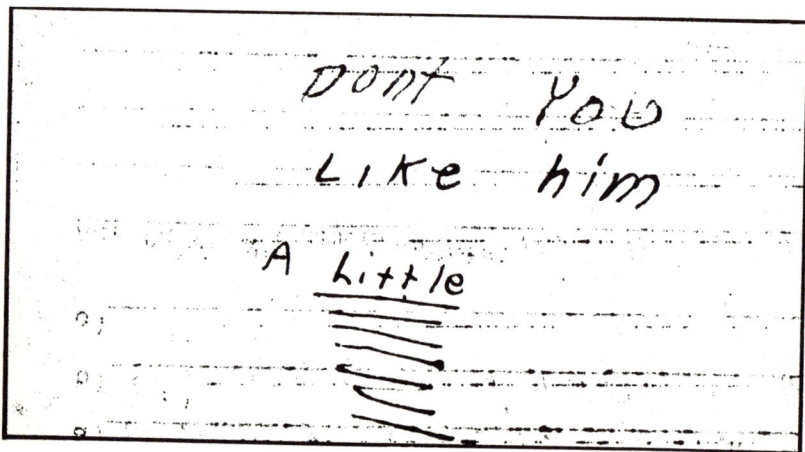

List the things that bother you most about grown-ups.

a) *Favoritism to brothers and sisters*

b) *Giving praise to a sister when she gets B's, no praise to you when you get a's*

c) *Forgetting to give you money when a tooth comes out*

D) *Not letting me make enough choices*

List three things you will always remember to do around children when you grow up.

a) *Be kind to them*

b) *Make them feel important by letting them talk*

c) *Talk about subjects that interest them.*

List three things you promise you won't say or do to kids when you grow up.

a) *Won't deprive them of things they want*

b) *Won't deprive them of the story about the birds and the bees*

c) *Won't deprive them of letting them go on dates*

List three things which really trouble you about being a child.

a) *Growing up in a war filled nation*

b) *Having all other members of my family killed, then being alone in the world*

c) *Not being able to go to the college of my choice*

Any further comments? *I had many other ideas for some parts, but could not write them because they weren't nice, especially for parts 2 & 3.*

Your Grade: 5 Your Age: 10

Above: A Fifth Grader with more ideas than he or she would reveal.

At left: Sometimes the back of a questionnaire gave us a glimpse of some extracurricular activity.

```
List the things that bother you most about grown-ups.
a) When grown-ups pry into your personal life which they
b) have no bussiness knowing.
c)

List three things you will always remember to do around children when you
grow up.
a)
```

Every gripe voiced in the lower grades is represented in Fifth Grade, but more noticeably present are questionnaires in which a child's answers say, in effect, "I'm ME!" Embarrassment is UP (see box score, page 42); the other items level off or taper off (*way* off in the matter of grownups' talking and telephoning). More of the standard complaints about *yelling, punishment,* being *bossed* and *pushed around* are qualified by the phrase **in front of people**— friends, company, guests, relatives, the public. There is a bloc increasingly concerned with justice and with what amounts to invasion of privacy—perhaps more sharply defined for this age grouping as a right to some thoughts and acts that grownups shouldn't interfere with. Don't be so nosy! Ease off a bit with the Grownup Power. Please, some more trust, attention, and effort at understanding us, if it isn't too much trouble.

Population is UP in Fifth Grade, forcing a modification in format† to make room for it. For fun and (hopefully) effect, let's stage an imaginary school-auditorium assembly. On stage: assorted faculty, school board, and other (PTA?) grownups. Enter Fifth Grade *via* center and side aisles. From the corridors and lobby off scene: some whispers, murmurs, snatches of talk:

. . . some are mean like uncles . . . Father talks about insurance and important bisness . . . They yell sometimes. Sometimes there kind . . . They conplain all the tine. Thay smoke to much. Thay drink to much . . . Acting dispising . . . Saying embarrassing things in public . . . You can't spend your money . . . Suspicious . . . Nagging . . . If you hurt yourself they act like you're going to die. They're cheap . . . If you are far behind in things they won't let you read or do anything else you want to . . . Think I'm a fragile china doll . . . Never want to play with you . . . Make you stay dressed up even after Church . . . Tell you not to do something, and then go do it themselves . . . Don't keep their promises . . . If we say it to them we're called rude . . . Ask if you are going to pass school or not . . . Some drink while driving . . . They said go on your to small to hang around with us so get out of here understand. That's what bothers me . . .

†Quotation of lines a) b) c) as normal sentences in paragraphs, instead of vertically, line-over-line.

The children are IN, and seated. Grownup in authority calls assembly to order, makes appropriate introductory remarks, suggests that **boys** and *girls* take turns in telling the assembly what bothers them . . .

Sitting next to a girl!

My Mom makes me say Hi to all the boys we see!

. . . about grownups.

They think they know everything. You can't stay up late. When they swear.

When they ask you about your boy friend and tease you because you do have one, and they think your to young.

They talk real long and when you think they're done they're only taking a breath. Sometimes they don't let you explain: No buts!

When you get hollered at in front of a friend. When you get hollered at for something your little brother did.

When someones over at night and they tell you go to bed. They tell you can't go with them. They say things you don't know about.

When I go somewhere grown-ups useally stop and talk for a while. When I go shopping with my mother she always looks around for a long time. Get hollered at in front of a friend.

They are always telling me not to smoke while there smoking. I cut an acre of lawn and get payed 5¢. Mom makes me drink my Coke in the kitchen. There to Bossy! . . .† Yeah! There to concerned about us when they should be concerned about themself.

Some grownups think you are little girls and baby you. Laughing at you when you make a mistake.

They tell us to go to bed early and we'll be rich, wealthy and wise and they stay up all night. They embarrass you in front of company. They forget their schools lessons just when you need help with your homework.

When I have friends over, Grown-ups tease me. My brother is always destroying my things. My sister is always (almost) slapping or hitting me . . . I don't like being bossed around.

They always yell at me. They won't let me have parties. They introduce to new friends at the wrong moment.

A few aren't very nice. When you try your best to help you do something wrong. They talk to other people about me.

†Leaders (. . .) indicate following material transcribed from "Any further comments?"

List the things that bother you most about grown-ups.
a) They make it sound like they are the
b) They are always asking questions like "How
c) Sometimes they treat you like a baby, like

List three things you will always remember to do around children when you grow up.
a) I will make them feel that they
b) I will make them feel comfortable by
c)

List three things you promise you won't say or do to kids when you grow up.
a) I won't cheat the one in the
b)
c)

Talking about me when I was a baby. Telling people what I've done. Telling people I don't do anything.

They say thing you don't want your Mother to know. They talk about how thin or Fat your getting. They always want to know everything . . . Yes! to help kids with there problems. Parents alway do the opposite of what you want. I want my hair Long aNd my Ma cuts it up to my ears.

They worry a lot. They're dumb. They don't give you your allowance.

They talk about you when there on the phone. They tease you. They complain about your work.

Grown-ups are always frantic about small things. My parents never tell me what its like to get maried. Everything gets blamed on me.

When your little sister or brother does something wrong and your mother blames it on you. When you axedently drop and break a glass and your mother tells the whole neighborhood.

There always drinking soda and don't leave any for you. When they eat pie and don't give you any. They don't let you go in the living room while talking with guests.

When you get something, and are about to say thanks a grown-up says "Say thanks." They're party-poopers! They clean out your room and throw valuable junk away . . . Yeah, thanks, S. Greene.

Always making kids do something. Always smoking and stuff.

> 1. a ultimate and you are just a servant.
> b. are you today when they know perfectly well what the answer will be. I don't object to this strongly and so sometimes I have an answer other than "Fine, thank you" but it still bugs me.
> c. you can't do a thing.
> 2. a. are grown-up and have equal rights as me.
> b. talking about things that they are bound to know about but that I am really interested in.

They yell at you when you don't do anything wrong. They ground you when you stay out and come in at 7:30 . . . When the styles are short your mother is so old-fashioned.

They know a lot more, and they really let us know. They won't let us eat anything before supper. They make us eat what we don't like.

When my Mother goes babysiting + she pays more attention to the kid than me. When my mother hits me + she says I probaly asked for it. When they hint around for you to leave.

They are always making you do jobs for them. Sometimes they make you do all the work while they just sit around and do nothing.

Boys! Girls! Kids! Just a minute . . .

I don't like to be called "kid!"

They should call you children, not kids.

Children! Ladies and gentlemen! We're glad to hear you say that because it never seemed to us that "kid" is right, either. Not for boys and girls your age. We'll try not to overdo it. Meanwhile, we were going to suggest that you try not all to speak at once. Ladies first. Girls, let's hear more from you . . .

Grownups act like we don't know anything. They seem to think when we find natures own things we aren't learning anything . . . I wish my best friends mother wouldn't keep her in the house in a "dress" all the time. (I hate dresses)

65

List the things that bother you most about grown-ups.

a) _Grown-ups expect so much of me._

b) _They won't let me alone._

c) _They won't let me do all the things I want to that are ok to do._

List three things you will always remember to do around children when you grow up.

a) _Have pateince._

b) _Try to help them_

c) _Try to let them do what they wish if it is okay to do_

List three things you promise you won't say or do to kids when you grow up.

a) _Gee, your dumb!_

b) _I can do this and you can't, Ha! Ha!_

c) _Get out of here and stop bothering me!_

List three things that really trouble you about being a child.

a) _Grown-ups are afraid your going to hurt_

b) _yourself doing something when you know_

c) _you can do it!!!_

Any further comments? _____

_____

_____

_____

Are you a boy?_____   Your Grade: _5_ Your Age: _10_
Or Girl? _X girl_

They show off when somebody come to the house. They're picky about what you wear. Every time you wear your hair a certain way they don't like it . . . And it troubles me you have to dress the way your parents want you to dress. You have to do what the teacher says even when your not her child. Everyone tell you what to do and you go nuts.

They act big. They do Kissing. They won't let you pick out your own clothes . . . They always have a ball but when you ask one thing they say no.

They say "Oh I understand" when they don't understand at all. They say "I don't care what other people do, you do what I tell you." "Now you're old enough to understand," they say, "that that dress is to short." And it isn't short at all . . . Well they won't let you play jumprope when they've promised someone else and I'd rather have 50¢ than 25¢ for allowance and I'd like two new dresses about every 5 months.

List the things that bother you most about grown-ups.

a) The idea that you must know what goes on when...
b) You should be in best manners when going out...
c) Being perfect!

List three things you will always remember to do around children when you grow up.

a) Be kind — get their friendship
b) Be humorus.
c) Give them new ideas on anything

List three things you promise you won't say or do to kids when you grow up.

a) Ask questions about their abilities
b) Give bad impressions
c) telling only one side of things

List three things which really trouble you about being a child.

(your ideas) a) Not being mean to someone I dislike
b) Not being looked upon by adults
c) Positions of the world

Any further comments? Yes, I will try to make people concreate and know how hard life is for negros or poor people

Your Grade: 5 Your Age: 10

All grown-ups think they are so big. They all have to have pretty clothes and hair. They don't understand us at all . . . They call me punk.

They act bigg. They do mushy things. They hit & scold a lot . . . I hate the way parents brag about their children. They say, "My children are really nice, they don't fight or they are not bad." Then when we are my father says take your brates out of here.

Teasing you about your Boy Friends some realy rub it in! Be able to Boss you around. Just cuse your the youngest in the family they call you the Baby . . . Parents think your to young to go steady.

They brag about themselves to much. They hardly ever play games with you. They don't spend enough time with you.

They always look at me when someone else is **making the noise.** They

67

always laugh at me. It seems to me that all they want **kids for is to scream at them** *. . . They embarass me the most when they laugh at* **me,** *or all stare at me when I dance.*

Right in front of my friends my parents say I've really slimmed down this year which gives them the idea I was fat. In public when my mother thinkes my hair neads to be combed she does it, and I'd rather do it my self. One time a teacher huged me for five minutes strait when I returned my sisters report card.

Girls, you've had the floor for some time now, and we see that the boys are just aching to top you—if they can. Won't those of you who still have your hands up try to be concise?

Grownups gossip too much. They are always going out to dinner.

When they're not feeling good they take it out on you.

Have to work more than my brothers.

Clerks in stores are afraid that kids are going to hurt something.

They go every place they wanna go. They are always saying how tired they are.

When they go to the bathroom it smells . . . They go and tell you to do something and then just sit around talking.

They don't listen to me.

They are always checking to see if you have brushed your hair always giving you heck for something you did not do.

They sometimes ignore you.

Smoking habits. Drinking habits. Swearing habits.

. . . 18 years old girls aways think there smart. They dress good.

Don't let us swear but when their mad they do. When they smoke it makes me cough. When around their friends their real nice but once they leave their mad again . . . If my sister hits me and I hit her back I get in trouble because I'm oldest. I don't really think it's fair.

. . . I don't think riots are right!

Boys act to big and emberis you sometimes.

They like to get you in trouble. They are don't understand kids.

. . . It is hard growing up when parents are mean to you.

They start bad habits for their children.

My parents call me bugy boo pom pom.

They get mad when you say something in slang but when you say it to your sister they laugh.

They are selfish. They are bossy. Act smart.

What could be more concise? Thank you, girls, thank you. Now . . .

They don't give you your allowence on time . . . People are alway bearing down on you. They don't trust you. They don't understand you . . . Yes, I hate being a kid!!!! H e l p !

That's very emphatic, young lady. Would you believe there are times when just being *alive* is enough to make anyone holler for help?

Now, do any of you men feel quite so put upon by grownups? Do you agree that some grownups are braggarts and showoffs?

Grownups think there realy tuff. And they hit you sometimes. They push you around.

They think there right all of the time.

Some grown-ups think that they are better then kids. Grown-ups ignor us when we try to tell them something. Another words they act like big shots.

They alway brag about how good we are. They punish us or hit us in front of people. They punish us for things we do not mean to do.

When one child gets in heck they are mad at everyone. Sometimes they are in favor of the girls when someone get in trouble. They brag about how great you are at something when you are not.

They sometimes brag to much. They make you take what you don't want or need. They just plain pester you.

They just plain pester you! Girls, don't you wish you'd said that? Men, you sound somewhat more exasperated than your sisters . . .

Always asking questions. Always acting smart. Think they're big . . . Yes, there's one thing I can't stand about grown-ups, they always go around acting smart because they're older and can drive a car and we can't.

Young man, since you've brought the matter up, let's pursue it. We can't help being older than you are, but are we to be envied because we can drive? . . .

Yes, the grow up are the pet's of the family. They get to drive the ski-doo. They get to drive dad's car. They get to go out on dat's.

Yeah, going out with girls. Driving a car. About have a accidents.

Don't have a lisence. Can't stay out late.

Your not big enough to have a car.

You cannot drive a car. There are too many rules for us to follow. There are too many things grown-ups can do we can't.

They steal from stores and steal cars. They race like a maniax, and they could hit somebody. Some boys think it's fun killing people . . . I have something to say about grown-ups. They think they are big but they aren't. I would fight a grown-up to protect myself if I am jumped.

Gentlemen, to save time let's wind up this matter of cars and driving with a show of hands. Two, three, five more. Thank you. We fear you will live to discover that car ownership and operation is a mixed blessing; there are certain expenses—certain and often. Maybe this is why grownups show off and "race like a maniax" sometimes—not that they should!

Boys, we do have a time limit to this assembly, but we'll hear all of you we can before the bell rings . . .

They don't let me shoot my B-B gun inside.

They always have to have their way. If kids do something wrong that would embarass them if someone told about, they tell about it, and get you embarassed. They won't play baseball with you.

Come Home at a certin time. Putting bike away. Practicing inserment.

Grown-ups don't like teenage groups. They think long hair for a boy is too far out. They don't like todays teen music . . . Grown-ups are too, too far out if they don't like mod groups.

They don't pay you when they promise you . . . I wish kids wouldn't copy my work.

List the things that bother you most about grown-ups.
a) _They think they are special_
b) _They get away with things_
c) _They have away with things_

List three things you will always remember to do around children when you grow up.
a) _not to whip them_
b) _act sweet_
c) _be kind_

List three things you promise you won't say or do to kids when you grow up.
a) _I won't be special_
b) _I will pay attention to them. I won't ignore them_
c) _I won't hit them_

List three things which really trouble you about being a child.
a) _We don't get privileges_
b) _We can't own stock_
c) _We can't work till twenty one_

List the things that bother you most about grown-ups.
a) *Why grownups say one thing and do another*
b) *Why do grownups smoke*
c) *Why do grownups drink*

List three things you will always remember to do around children when you grow up.
a) *Be nice to all kids white or negro.*
b) *Be nice to children but don't overdo it*
c) *try not to embarrass children*

List three things you promise you won't say or do to kids when you grow up.
a) *Call kids names*
b) *Be mean to kids*
c) *Be bossy because your older*

List three things that really trouble you about being a child.
a) *getting pushed around*
b) *Never going anywhere.*
c) *going to bed at 8:00*

Any further comments? *Yes, why are grownups fighting wars when working together we could be on the moon or even Mars.*

Are you a boy? *yes*

Grade: *5* Your Age: *11*
Or Girl? ___

When they acuse me of doing something I didn't do. When they egnore me when I try to tell or ask them something. They don't treat me fairly.

They have to know EVERYthing about the things you know. You have to tell them the marks you get in school. Sometimes they can't control their temper.

The fact that they never answer why I can't or have to. They won't let me argue when I know I'm right.

They never almost have time for us. They expect to much of you at an early age. They have you recite in front of visiters...People ask "where did you go?", "are your hands clean?"

Tell you to do before you did something else. Tell you what to do and to go. Makeing you do things when your tired.

When they tell you to work and everything and they keep at you. When they hit and when you do something bad it hurts. Why they make you do your homework right when you get home.

I think grown-ups are jumpy. Sometimes they worry too much. Thier're emotional . . . Nobody cares if you're a kid or not.

71

They call me "my little boy" instead of just "my son." They don't let you do things your own way even when your way is better. You can't do the fun things grownups can do . . . KIDS AREN'T ALL BAD!

On this ringing note let it be imagined that the period bell sounds, ending the mock assembly. As the Fifth Grade troops out of the hall to its classrooms, we overhear . . .

They make you feel wrong.

Could *any* age be more precise about the discomfiture of embarrassment?

One other minor complaint from a Fifth Grade boy was: **They won't tell thier age.** No? Well, one of "thier" ages can be guessed, because, we dare say, no kid—sorry, no *child*—of fifty years ago would have boasted that . . .

My pchiatrist, Dr. R-----, is a better pchiatrist than you. ^{eccuse spelling}

List the <u>things</u> that <u>bother</u> you <u>most</u> about <u>grown-ups.</u>
a) *They pay more attention to other grown ups than to kids.*
b) *Sometimes they overdue it when they get mad at us.*
c) *They make you practice the piano every day.*

List three things you will always remember to do around children when you grow up.
a) *I will always be friendly to children, notice them.*
b) *I will never flip my lid if I am disturbed with them.*
c) *I will let them decide for themselves whether or not they would enjoy taking lessons and then make them practice.*

List three things you promise you won't say or do to kids when you grow up.
a) *I won't say "Oh, what a sweet boy (or girl) you are! * sigh * "*
b) *I won't pull their hair (or my hair) when I'm mad at them.*
c) *I will not be a teacher!*

List three things that really trouble you about being a child.
a) *I'm not old enough to fly airplanes or helicopters.*
b) *I'm not old enough to drive a car.*
c) *You can't vote.*

Any further comments? *I'm not really complaining, but I would like to be an adult and be on top of things!*

CHAPTER VI

WHAT BOTHERS SIXTH GRADE MOST ABOUT GROWNUPS

Ages Eleven and Twelve

Someone

Guess Who?

? ! ⊚ ; . ? ? ⊚ ! ;

Anonomus

EARLIER IN THIS BOOK we calculated that the returned questionnaires presented a potential 18,930 lines of comment. We pulled a boner. The number is incorrect (should be 18,390) but we let it stand so that the children quoted on pages 120 and 121 will know that they're in the company of a fellow fumbler with figures. Sixth Grade represents another 30 percent of our responders and tops them all in linage used—enough to fill a hundred pages of this book if all were quoted and printed line-for-line without stopping. This is a conservative estimate.

Of Sixth Grade 46 percent answered Questions 1 through 4 conscientiously, using up lines *a)-b)-c)* completely, writing often into the margin and sometimes beyond. This is the grade of the overflowing questionnaire, and material sufficient for a veritable "Child's Garden of Any Further Comments." We are hearing from boys and girls who, at ages 11, 12, and 13, may well have attained up to 75 percent of the vocabulary, reading comprehension, and general school achievement to be expected of them at 18.†

Any further comments? **A lot of kids have new modern clothes—clothes that follow the style. I'm not saying I don't have new clothes, it's just that the ones I have don't follow the styles. I might say, "So and so has this," and my parents say, "I don't care what · · · PLEASE SEE BACK · · · · ·**

†"A Child's Mind," p. xxi

· · · So and so has. Your my child!" Then I might add, **"But stick out like a sore thumb."** Then I get hit.

The temptation, with such graphic material as this on hand, is to use it all. But this would crowd out some of the Sixth Grade's cogent shorter remarks, such as the answer to Question 1, line *b*), below, which is one for grownups to remember along with that Fifth Grader's **They make you feel wrong** (page 72). Also, if pressed to find *one* remark that can stand as the sense of the meeting for *all* Sixth Grade, it would be hard to improve on the same young lady's answer to Question 4.

This chapter will attempt to anthologize, so to speak, the things that Sixth Graders say bother them most about grownups, with the assurance that they are well represented also in other chapters of this book.

List the things that bother you most about grown-ups.

a) *They're not very trusting*

b) *When I feel bad about something I've done they make me feel worse*

c) *When they believe someone else's lies when I'm telling the truth*

List three things you will always remember to do around children when you grow up.

a) *Instead of criticizing I will try to help them*

b) _____

c) _____

List three things you promise you won't say or do to kids when you grow up.

a) *I won't say, absolutly no*

b) _____

c) _____

List three things that really trouble you about being a child.

a) *I like being a child but I don't like for grownups to*

b) *make me feel limited because I am a child.*

c) _____

Any further comments? _____

_____

_____

_____

Are you a boy?____   Your Grade: 6 Your Age: ____
                      Or Girl? X

74

Though it is not exclusively a Sixth Grade practice, many of the children use Question 4 as an extension of Question 1. Therefore, some of the following quotations are taken indiscriminately from both sources, and in some cases condensed or summarized. Our aim is to provide a faithful *context* for the **boldface** transcription of a child's own words. Now and again a youngster bursts the bounds of Question 1 — just like outgrowing his clothes. As a prime example of this, here is . . .

1.a) **Well they give you lecters and try to make you just perfect.**

b) **They force you into doing things. (? ! @ !)**

c) **They don't know music and think they do and make you do them over and over.**

d) **They think your a baby and make you take naps and go to bed early etc.**

e) **They think you'll get sick eating cake and than get close and smoke. (uck)**

f) **Sometimes when your on a trip and when you were gone they had a number of things so you try to explain and they say, well you should have finished it. (o o o o)**

4.a) **You get picked on.**

b) **Everybody butt's in front of you in the grocery line.**

5. **Grown ups don't understand the younger generation. The striks going on are to show that we're okay. They think the Y. G. is crazy well look at the crazy things they do.**

Since we have a music expert here (*1.c*) let's say, *à la* Count Basie, once more once . . .

1.a) **They always tell you to do something like clean your pets cage or s right when your doing things like playing two square, baseball, basketball, or tetherball and they make you do it right away and your fiends have to go home.**

b) **They will never play any games with you like chess, checkers, or cards when your in the mood to.**

c) **They never let you have your fiend overnight.**

d) **They don't let you join groups like swim club, tumbeling, and art programs.**

4.a) **They don't let you me have my own room.**

b) **They always look at you as though you've done something bad.**

c) **They don't let you go down town ever by yourself.**

Turn your personal time clock back to ages 11 and 12. Try to recapture the indignity of being made to **take naps** or never being allowed to have a special **fiend** visit you overnight.

Doesn't anybody yell at age-11-to-12 boys and girls? Or boss and push

List the things that bother you most about grown-ups.

a) Some Grown-ups treat children like babies

b) Some Adults expect children to understand everyth

c) Some Adults act superior and sophisticated around children.

List three things you will always remember to do around children when you grow up.

a) Never under-estimate their imagination.

b) Be patient and understanding.

c) Try and bring myself down to their level.

List three things you promise you won't say or do to kids when you grow up

a) I won't tease them because of their childishw

b) " " try to shelter them from hardships.

c) " " try to make them mature before their ready to.

List three things which really trouble you about being a child.

a) It's hard to understand things which your parents k   from

b) It's hard to accept the responsibility's of an adul

✱ but not get any privliges

Any further comments?

_____

_____

_____

Examples of most and least among Sixth Graders. Below—probably "just one of those days" for this boy or girl—the only response of its kind received.

Grade: 6 Your Age: 12

Any further comments?

I can't think of anything to say

Grade: _six_ Your Age: 12

76

~~clarification of red~~
moments about 1, 2 + 3

Some adults treat 12yr. olds like babies,
ney shelter them, and expect them to' live a
hetered life, naturally, this is impossible.
'aṛents who shelter their children are
eing cruel. If you go to school with
lo other children, you cannot live a
completely shelterd life, so if your
~~parents~~ think your a baby, but you
really aren't, you envy other girls who
are treated their age.

comment on 4.
I find it hard to be a child, because
nost of the girls in my class are treated like
.dults. I think ~~my~~ my parents have higher
tandards then most other parents, and
t's hard to be good when everybody
else is allowed to do things that you
aren't. I have to take most of the
hardships of an ▬▬▬ teenager, (12yr.)
but not get the privlages. It's hard,
▬▬▬▬▬▬▬▬▬▬▬▬▬▬▬▬▬

them around, and hit them? There are a hundred-odd questionnaires stating
that somebody does (including other kids who are **acting to big and always
want to fight**). Still, as with the Fifth Graders, there is a tapering-off of the intensity of the cries. Just one Sixth Grader bottomed off a questionnaire be-
wailing his or her lot in such rock-bottom terms as these:

They are to mean to us poor helpless children

With reference to the box score on page 42, objection to grownups' smoking trends UP again among these older children, the effect only slightly beclouded by two or three who wish that they, too, could smoke. Are Sixth Graders underprivileged? Yes, in the sense that . . .

I can't have the privligages *that* older people can

. . . or as analyzed in the questionnaire reproduced on the preceding page. Whatever statistical sense can be made of these Sixth Grade reports, the push toward adulthood is so evident you can almost feel it.

Boy, 12: Objecting to grownups' control over him, and silly rules:

if you make a mistake you get landed on, But if they make a mistake its all right

at the movies your considered a gron-up

yet at a restrunt you get a child's por stion

get made fun of if you even look at a girl

Girl, 12½: Griped because she can't have someone over when left by herself for a couple of hours, and . . .

If you talk back to them they say they don't want to hear that kind of talk from you then they get mad and say things you don't like to hear.

They think they are better than you but, "All men are created equel."

I can't have my privacy when I want it.

I can't make up my own mind about things like what dress I should wear.

A child can't vote or drive but <u>some</u> of us might do ~~thees~~ these things better than 21 year olds . . . I enjoyed this very much.

Age 12: A victim of teasing, getting picked on, adult show-offism, and . . .

They always fuss with your clothes or something.

I am 12 yrs. old and I don't like to be called a child.

I don't like to be called a little kid.

And I don't like to be treated like a child.

. . . And when at home I don't like to have anyone to tell me to hurry. I like to take many pain with my work.

Girl, 11: With a sneer for grownups who say how you've grown when they haven't seen you, and for blaming the oldest when the youngest did it . . .

They act very odd in front of a hippie

It really troubles me to have grownups around

Grownups never let you have privacy

I'd rather be a child that can do what Grown-ups do

. . . Yes, I don't like grown-ups They never let you do anything I wish I could   D   R   I   V   E !

P. S. I don't like questionaires.

Boy, "almost 12:" Glumly looks forward to . . .

. . . at 12 you pay like grown-up but aren't treated like one.

Girl, 12: Bossed around, told what to do and wear; has the "can't drive" blues.

Since I'am the only girl I do more work than my 2 brothers.

I'am 12 I think I should have more rights, and priviledges. Instead of haveing to stay home and work. Also my mother says I can never babysit I think I should. At least when I'am 14 or so.

Age 11: Oppressed by "a certain time" put upon his coming home, and "a silent treatment" form of punishment imposed by angry grownups.

IT TAKES SO LONG TO GROW UP
I WANT TO BE MORE INDEPENDENT
I WANT MORE FREEDOM OF CHOISE (I'M LOOKING FORWARD TO THIS)

Girl, 12: Grownups don't understand; troubled by boys, and wondering if perhaps she ought to be more of a tomboy . . .

. . . I like being a child only I can't wait till I am a about 16 years old.

Girl, 12: Protesting grownups' tattling and devotion to the telephone, troubled because of small stature, and therefore . . .

. . . about getting the right size bra.

From a boy or girl of no stated age comes this simplest of final comments:

. . . I want to grow up.

There is an appreciable number who "think adult" in terms of **I can't work in a factory, can't earn and spend my own money**; also, **we can't vote.** One underprivileged loner (**I'd rather play alone by my self than have a friend around**) may need to be resold later on the democratic process:

I never seem to get anything I want. The other kids always vote for something that I don't want. If I want a horse they vote for a ski-doo.

"I love Girls"  "I hate girls"

In the tug of war between boys and girls, three outspoken young men of ages 11 through 13 (collectively bothered by grownups' overpraise, yelling, slapping, inconstancy, plus **big guys push you around** and bossy, ugly, slave-driving, big-mouthed adults) put in the strongest words since Fourth Grade on a certain subject . . . **I'm not getting married.**

I am not getting married!

I IS NOT Geting Marryed

. . . the one in the middle making darn sure we get the message by adding, **"In other words, I am going to be a bachelor."**

There are no girls reporting in against marriage. In some 40 forms touching on male-female relationships, the sexes divide evenly on sensitivity to teasing by grownups about one's boy or girl friend; also, as best we can tell, on things like dates, can't have, and dances, can't go to. A couple of girls are resentful of grownups' "NO" to boy-girl parties and, alas . . .

Most of the cute boys fall for older girls.

You can't kiss boys. You can't go anywheres with them.

My mom says I'm not old enough to have boy-girl parties and that I won't be until I'm in nineth grade.

I want to do things (pierce my ears) but mom says no and I tell her their my ears but she says I'm a little kid and is supposed to mind.

In view of the controversy over sex education (home *vs.* school and/or church), we wondered if anything from our young ones (in all grades) would put some words in edgewise from the children's point of view. At these ages, not yet, we conclude; but parents and others coping with Sixth Graders may wish to note the following:

I don't think [this is a 12-year-old boy speaking] **parents talk enough about the facts of life. I know most of them, but my parents don't know that. I think they should tell fairly soon, so they know that I know them.**

A girl, same age, comments . . . **Yes! one very, (I think thing) important thing is, not many girls' or boys' parents sit down with them and talk —→ to them about "growing up." I think it is wonderful to be a child. But it is even more fun "Growing Up" into an adult.**

Actually, there is no frame of reference informing us that these young ones are talking about biology at all, either the ones just quoted or the Age 12 reproduced on page 22, or the boy and girl following, both 11-year-olds:

They wait too long to tell you things.

Grown-ups seem to not let you know about things you should

1.b) **How are babies brought to the world** [asks another boy, 11, questioning also why grownups get "atvatages" of things.] This questionnaire concludes soberly: **Frort a man to go out and earn a living for his wife. But for the wife to have moor than one child at a time. A grown up has a lot of responsibility.**

From back on page 39 we *re*quote: **"I think this is the silliest thing I've ever heard of. Why do you ask such crazy questions?"** The least we can do for

†This word not clearly written. It could be also read as "Your."

this fulminatory critic is to let the numerous questioners of Sixth Grade put a questionnaire to us, with the assistance of an Age 11 from Fifth Grade (identified by * * below; see also page 71).

Why they put you on the spot.

Why when you know when your right they think of some way to get out of it.

Why do they kill people on the streets.

How come parents can do things that children can't. like go out to eat.

Why does a teacher make you do work you don't want to do.

How come a grown up person can have previgles to go places and do many more things that a child of 12-15 cannot do. Like having your parents treat you like a baby.

. . . Why can't children decide what is good for them instead of the parents?

Why can't I go to dances at the age of 12.

How come mothers hit us without knowing the story or what goes on?

Do they have to work real hard?

Is it ok for a parent to help with homework?

Is it ok for a grownup to leave a child?

When do we start baby sitting?

teachers why canned we go out doors after school at night. we did not do anything wrong.

*Why grownups say one thing and do another?

*. . . Yes, why are grownups fighting wars when working together we could be on the moon or even mars?

Why they argue so much?

Children seem to be able to settle arguments why can't adults.

How come they smoke?

How come they treat us like this?

Why they do so many bad things?

Why kids have such a big burden?

Why we are bothered so much?

Why people drink alcohol?

When [why] they keep asking questions when you ans[wer] them several times.

In case some of us teacher types are tempted to insert question marks in various proper places above, look first at our own questionnaire. If defined as "a set, or list, of questions" (as dictionaries indeed do define questionnaire), what must the kids think we think we're doing? How come *we* didn't use the interrogative wording: *Can you* list the things, etc., etc., question mark? With sharp young eyes watching out for adult performance gaps, we can't be too careful. From answers to Question 1:

Parents ball you out for doing something wrong then they turn around and do it and youcan'tsay anything about it.

Some parents smoke and drinkinfrontof you and then say not to smoke or drink.

They pick at you to stop a habit when they have the same bad habit.

They are always telling us kids not to smoke & they go & smoke.

Parents scold me for wrong-doing then they turn around and do the same thing you did. I can't say anything about it or I'll get hit.

Either they expect you to be irresponsible or completely responsible.

List the things that bother you most about ~~grownups~~.

a) They don't relize the things we don't want to do
A) EXAMPLE They make you take a shower. Drive in car.
B) THEY use phsycology at the wrong time. (THEY put you on the spot and make you ADMIT you did SOMETHING wrong. OVD

List three things you will always remember to do NOT around children when you grow up.

a) Not to SPANK OR pinch cheeks often BECAUSE it makes them hate you.
b) Not to exagerate things I WOULDN'T TELL THEM THE HOUSE[IS]ON FIRE ON TILL THEY ARE OUTSIDE OUT [I] would TELL THEM THAT FIRE IS BAD AND CAN KILL WILL

List three things you promise you ~~will~~ WILL say or do to kids when you grow up.

a) _____

b) _____

c) _____

List three things which really trouble you about being a child.

a) YOU'RE TREATED TO YOUNG, YOUR cute
b) little, weak, stupid, KID
c) _____

On the overleaf of this vehement questionnaire, response to 1.c) illustrates "performance gap" in these words: THEY TELL YOU NOT TO DO SOMETHING THEN THEY DO IT AND WENE YOU TELL THEM THEY SAY DON'TALK BACK

The parents want you to follow in their footsteps, but they don't want you to cuss, or smoke

When my mother tells me to do something and my father tells me I don't know what to do first and if I don't do the thing my father says he gets mad and my mother gets mad if I don't do what she says

They say things are perfect when they really aren't.

They often say you're such an angel but you aren't.

Your parents say you can go over to your friend's house then they forget where you are and then when they find you they punish you

They make little thing seem like you murdered President Johnson

They answer yes but sound mad

They think your too young to do one thing and to old to do an other

They yell at you when your on the phone and tell you not to gossip but when they get on the phone they gossip for hours.

We show respect for them while they show none for us.

Sometimes they think they know things they didn't even study in school.

They are too upsetable. They don't care about a lot of important matters, but they care greatly about local matters.

One minute they say not to come in and the next minute they yell because you didn't come in . . . I wish they'd just tell you what you did wrong.

From answers to Question 4:

You are expected to take responsibilities, but you aren't always allowed to have the privilages that go with them . . . Sometimes grownups don't try to the best of their abilities to understand kids.

lending money and they don't pay it back

My mother goes to school and says → she hasn't any money to buy me anything, but she buys herself a lot of unnecisary things.

If I go to thee movies I have → to find my own money to spend, but when I invite a friend their mother gives them the money.

Why they put a lot of makeup on their face
Why they yell at other people for putting it on

Parents tell you not to do something and you turn and they do it . . . Yes, Parents tell you "no you cant" But don't tell me why not he say "Non of your buniness"

You're old enough to know better but young enough to do it anyway

No youre not old enough, No you're to young $^{\text{we get mixed terrible because}}_{\text{of tha}}_{\text{t}}$

From "any further comments?":

Parents say when they yell at you that means they love you but with some parents its different.

In addition to **They Smoke** and **They drink Alcoholic Beverages,** a boy complains, **"They don't care about wildlife."** He is almost alone among all the children in observing and commenting on such performance gaps as . . .

Adults don't care about things like a bird with broken wing or if a small pet dies like a mouse or rat. Some don't even care about nature. on my way up mt. W-------- Trail I see them trowing rocks and droping litter.
Some Adults even steal and murder!

From the same classroom (unidentified as to grade†) comes one of the rare questionnaires that say anything about religious experience . . . **in church I hear a song — and I cry — and this lady said I was just close to my Heavenly Father** . . . and his or her answer to *4.a)* is:

parts of our religion — when he/comes agian — I have lots of questions.
(The Lord)

Remember what He said when certain grownups tried to push children around in His presence. He inquired also: "What man is there of you, whom if his son ask bread, will he give him a stone?" Not a word about bread from any of our respondents **(They hardly ever have hamburgers!)** nor more than a whisper that children here and there may be underfed, but there is mounting pressure for a glimpse of the jewel of truth in adult-child relationships. This is another percentage upswing that Sixth Grade imparts to the pattern.

They have a habit of falsely acusing children.
Parents alway stick-up for another child not their own.

They acuse you of things and they keep rubbing it in.

They think any thing I say is a lie and it is not

Two people do something and one said the other did it and they believe it and he gets in trouble.

When they give you heck when maybe they now who did it and don't say

Sometimes they will punish me for things my little brother lied about before I tell my side.

Few listen to both sides of a fight and say that the one they like best is telling the troth.

Parents should not hold secrets away from you or be so worried about you. Parents should not lie for our own good

†But entirely in the Sixth Grade manner, overflowing questionnaires and all.

List the things that bother you most about grown-ups.

a) When they shout at you for nothing

b) When you get blamed for something you didn't do

c) They get mad awfully easy

List three things you will always remember to do around children when you grow up.

a) Be nice to them.

b) Give them some attention.

c) Give them something to keep them occupied

List three things you promise you won't say or do to kids when you grow up.

a) Won't tell them there is no such thing as

b) Santa Claus and the Easter Bunny and

c) the tooth fairy

List three things which really trouble you about being a child.

a) You can't do what the other guys do

b) You must have permission to do mostly

c) everything

Any further comments? Most kids that turn into mean teenagers is because because of lack of attention

Your Grade: 6   Your Age: 11

Lest we forget, there is a body of Sixth Grade basic indignation erupting in the unadorned manner of the lower primary grades . . .

1.a) hollering

b) They don't understand me

c) I don't understand them

4.a) getting up in the morning

b) everybody's teasing

c) everybody's hollering   —*Girl, 12*

. . . but the pivotal resentment of these older ones — trending upward from Fourth Grade on — was voiced by an Age 12, right on target as follows:

**They don't ever shut up about things I did when I was a baby
. . . Please don't treat us like babies. We really aren't you know**

"**They protect you like mother hen,**" squawks an Age 11. "**When you get about 14 they still thing you wear diapers,**" protests another Age 12, again a girl, among some dozens of youngsters saying, in effect, the same.

85

"You would think," sighs a young lady (whom we think really wanted the word "Who" instead), "that Grownup's were once our age." She listed **Growing up to be Like Them** as one of her "troubles" and freighted her questionnaire with such a mixture of 12-year-old "bother" that it might as well lead a final selection of Sixth Grade woe:

Every thing has-to-be right the First time.
Eat all that she makes, even if it's not good Food.
She's the boss, she thinks, but Dad Knows better.

Sometimes they don't relie on you and you know you can do it

Being sheltered and hided from the world
Being forced to make a decision before having thouroughly aware of both sides

There talking about something then when you walk in they stop.

Won't let you swear when they do it all the time

When they say how good they were when they were children

they always are referring to when they were little.
they don't understand its now not 40 years ago.

Think they are big. And children don't have a right to live.

Their always talking about stuff like disapline.

Some are too strict and beat their children.
Some are too easy on their children and don't care what they do.
Some won't let their children face life's facts until it is to late.

They don't listen, it's just like talking to a wall.

They make you clean the house while they sleep

There has to be a halt to this somewhere, or there would be half-a-bookful of Sixth Grade alone. So let it be here, with thanks to all for their good company and questionnaires ranging from **no theres nothing to say good about grown-ups** to **Thank you for asking these questions.**

CHAPTER VII

THINGS WHICH REALLY TROUBLE US ABOUT BEING A CHILD

List the things that bother you most about grown-ups.

a) _yell at me._

b) _send us to bed to early_

c) _make us make our own bed._

List three things which really trouble you about being a child.

a) _my brothers_

b) _my bratty cousins,_

c) _my mother + my father_

Any further comments? _my mother + father are always bothering me every single day._

Your Age: _11_

IN RETROSPECT—and could it be this kind of wisdom after the fact that the children mean when they say, **"They think they know everything"**?—it might have been better tactics to put the question, *List three things which really trouble you about being a child,* second instead of fourth in order. It is complementary to "the things that bother you most" and we've wandered into this territory already in pursuit of boys and girls who, on their own initiative, used it as an extension of, or annex to, Question 1. Having answered all previous questions in detail, one Sixth Grade boy stated his three troubles to be: **"I can't answer questionaires."** Forms with no reply and those with only one-line responses add up to a quarter of our boys and girls, Question-4 dropouts, so to speak—and it could be for no more reason than lack of time or, better yet, lack of trouble!

The material in this chapter stems from less than 50 percent of the questionnaires. Why not more? First, the no-reply "dropouts" noted above. Then we found out right away that what really troubles a sizable bloc of boys and girls is—school! This appeared to be intriguing enough to save for separate consideration, together with the early-to-bed syndrome in combination with still another factor. A quantity of the forms proved to be of a kind we labeled "repeaters," questionnaires offering little more than a restatement throughout of a child's original complaints, as in this representative sample from an Age 10:

List the things that bother you most about grownups.

a) **Thay   slap in the face.**

b) **Thay   spank me.**

c) **Our teacher is mean**

List three things you will always remember to do around children when you grow up

a) **do not slap them.**

b) **do not spank them.**

c) **do not   holler at them.**

List three things you promise you won't say or do to kids when you grow up.

a) **slap them.**

b) **spank th em.**

c) **holl er at them.**

List three things which really trouble you about being a child.

a) **They slap in the face.**

b) **They   spank me.**

c) **They   holler at   us.**

For a quick consensus of what really troubles the children, we noted the one-line responses from two grades to see what would turn up. From Third Grade . . .

I don't like   school

Im to small

H e r e i n g   m y   m o t h e r a n d F a t h e r yell.

I would n't   have   to   go   to   school.

older kids push around.

My bigge s t s i s t e r h o l l ers a t m e

They don't let you stay home alone.

I would like to be stronger

I get blame on evey thing.

You can not do anything you want.

they don,t take   me   wait then.

an older brother

Daddy and Mother said that you can not do that you are to small.

gr o wup b e a t us.

We can't do what we want.

to do my arithmetic

There is only one thing that bothers me. I can't voat.

The only thing that I dont like about being a child is that you cant do what you want.

Fifth Grade, too, has a laconic group whose members state in a line or less their troubles in regard to school (9); can't do, get, go, or have what they want (8); the tyranny of older children (8); being bossed or pushed around (6); denial or limitation of motorcycle and hot rod privileges, driving, horses and bikes (4); inadequacies of age and size (3); early bedtime (3); and miscellaneous miseries on the order of . . .

Weeding the garden
not letting /̸/ me   explan̸
Parents always have to know everything →that's going on.
you can't go dancing
You get screamed at a lot
Your parents alwas baby you.
Can't ever go hunting.
Don't have a lot of money =to= to spend
controling my temper
People call you names
Grownups bug ya.
I'm the oldest so I have to take care of my sisters.
Your always have to do work

These Third and Fifth Grade quick answers project once more the straitjacketed world that children live in, that place of limits as described by Dr. Schroeder. One after-image produced by reading the questionnaires in bulk is that in answers to Question 4 the children tend more to particularize their grievances. This is the area in which we who are separated by decades from the childhood condition get our sharpest reminders of what it is like.

"The fact that you are littler than others"

FROM DOZENS of Question 4 responses the phrases **being so small, I do not like to be small, being littel, to be short,** and **I am not strong enough** pull us back into the pre-teen years when so much of everything was bigger, older, more powerful, and at times even smarter than we were. There are vivid ela- borations on the theme. We quote from all grades, and in *italic* type when we are certain that a girl is speaking.

Well, for one thing your small, and when you do something that the grown-ups think is funny, but you didn't mean it to be funny

I am small and everyone critisizes me. I am thin also.

having big feet. bieng small. Not being able to swear.

You can't reach things.
Bigger kids always wants to fight.
There are things we can't do.

89

You have to stand in chairs to reach cupboard.
I can't run so fast with short legs.

You are small and can't reach some things.

Ah, but a man's reach *should* exceed his grasp, as Browning wrote, but what Heaven† hath a youngster in such a fix as . . .

I can't reach the glasses to get a drink
There's nothing to eat for a snack
I'm too big for my chair
I.m never tall enough.
I don't get to spank anyone.

I don't like to be small and have old child pick on me

Bigger people pick on me	**I don't grow much**
Work is harder	**I weigh the same**
Big people run fast	**and I can't catch a kik – ball**

I wish I was big so I could be the boss
Try to ride a bike.   Being so small.

Grown-up call you little puanks.
They all say you are too small.
They call me punk.

Being small.	**My father and mother slap me**
Not being to defend yours self.	**I have to look up to tall people**
Geting p u sh ed around.	**You have to go to school**

You have to have a boady gard

You are too small to understand ^some things
You are too small to do some things

not being able to be smart enough for fam ~~ilies~~ talkings

One of the most emphatic of all the "too small" remarks is this from the questionnaire reproduced on page 28:

4.*a)* **I am to small and I want to**
  b) **be biger than my sister!**
  c)

Any further comments?   **one more thing my sister**
        is a stupid sister

. . . and thus we leap from the frying pan of Small Size into the fiery pandemonium of Sibling Rivalry.

---

†When Robert Browning wrote these thoughts, his own son was probably just a toddler.

Big Brother; Big Sister

OR BOTH. We brought together 80-odd forms bearing on this problem (and the problem of older kids in general, of whom more later) and quote them at some length for the benefit of the "only children" in the audience. Children and adults who have had to cope only with cousins and such are indubitably less persecuted. Also, they do not have the amazement of discovering in later years that brothers and sisters very often turn out to be splendid people, helpful and good company. Here, then, is vicarious experience for them, beginning with a Master or Miss Age 11 whose a)-b)-c) of real trouble reads . . .

> **my sister**   **my brother**   **my stepsister**

Others pile on the details. A Miss Age 8, who has previously pointed out that **some kids never see much of their parents,** offers . . .

> *Big sisters have their boy friends over*
> *Big brothers have girl friends over*
> *Many times kids are lonesome*

"Older brothers, older sisters," writes a boy, 12, but he makes a further comment tell more of the story . . .

> **Yes, It hurts when you get (killed), by brothers but I am glad I am still here.**

Boys aged 8, 10, and 11½ respectively, report:

> **My brother Stealing my papers**
> **My mother ask me question**
> **My Sister cuts my papers**

> **I don't get so many privileges as my older brothers and sisters.**

> **When a sister or brother come home for vacation from college you feel left out.**

Summing up for the prosecution, boys and girls *vs.* sisters, there's such comment as . . .

> **older sister boss me a around**
> **si ster's say not ' y thing's**
> **sister 's s ay too much**

> *My sister hits me*
> *She makes me pick up*
> *She yells at me*

> **You bring a friend up to play and you have to work, but when /**
> **You get shoved around all the time.**
> **Your older sisters blame you for doing something**
>   **you never did. .**

> sister brings someone home she don't have to work.

I have a hard time trying to ask my sistersomething

Wash dishes.

Listen to my sister on ~~the dro=~~ *the drums.*

Listen to rock en roll ~~mùc~~ *music.*

My Big sister GO's to bed late and I GOt TO GO earlyier

being shove around by my sisters

Any older people boss me around

All my older sisters & brothers get what ever

My older sister makes me do everything   they want.

when your sister is sick and you have to do the dishes

Having a sister that kicks you all the time and your parents
don't do any thing about it.

your mother and father aren't fair in fights

my sister gets a lot more candy than you do

You are to little.

You get hit by your big sister.

You get picked up and thrown into the lake.

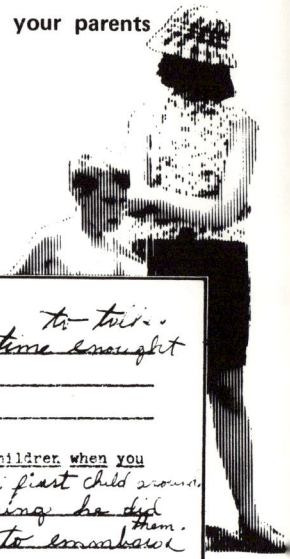

List the things that bother you most about grown-ups.

a) *They don't always give you time enought to thi..*

b) _____

c) _____

List three things you will always remember to do around children when you
grow up.   *not do I would not blame it on the first child arou..*

a) *If a child is accused of doing anything he did*

b) *Be careful not to say anything to emmbaraw them.*

c) *Let them have time to tell.*

List three things you promise you won't say or do to kids when you grow up.

a) *I will not embarass them....*

b) *I will not blame it on the first child*

c) *I will always give them time to tell, anything the plea.*

List three things which really trouble you about being a child.

a) *Grownups are bigger and able to say*

b) *That they would'nt get mad you*

c) *for something you did'nt do.*

Any further comments? _____

List the things that bother you most about grown-ups.

a) They yell too much

b) They smoke

c) They make you eat food you don't like

List three things you will always remember to do around children when you grow up.

a) Not to use bad language

b) Make them do their homework

c) _____

List three things you promise you won't say or do to kids when you grow up.

a) Not to spank them hard

b) Not to use bad english

c) _____

List three things which really trouble you about being a child.

a) Parents don't let us watch enough T.V.

b) Children can't yell back at parents

c) _____

Any further comments? My sister bugs me to much. Sometime she is going to get belted

Compare "any further comments," above, with the sisterly sentiments expressed on page 44. Now, for some views of Big Brother as Big Trouble, begin with the following. This is an Age 11½ reporting, but no certainty on whether a boy or a girl is the source (though we favor the latter):

Having to be bossed around by your older brothers.
To be hit everytime when you go in your brothers room.
Being left home with my brothers alome.

Any further comments? **Yes — My brothers are a big pest every day.**
They pick on me to. I wish I had a sister. — but she would have to
be younger than me.

Two Age 12s, an 11, and a 10—all girls—report:

My oldest brother gets more Priviledges than I.
Since I'am the only girl I do more work than my 2 brothers.
We are bossed arounds. They always tell us what to do.

My brother always gets to go places and I never do.

93

My brother is always telling me what to do

Your older brothers teese you a lot

. . . and here are two views from kid brothers, both 10-year-olds:

My brother pushes me around.

And my brother makes me do everything.

I can't go to any games with my brother.

These are representative, likewise the following from both sexes:

Your bigger brother always pounding on you

Your bigger brother always telling you what to do

big brothers

getting pushed and bossed from big brothers

Doing extra chores for my brother.

When your brother slaps you

When your brother gits you about being a child

When your brother would *(sic)* let you go with him

Get kick by my father.

When you get pushed around by my brother.

My brothers don't let me go to games with them! Sports

if you have a big brother he starts fights

Push. Pound. Slap. Boss. Naw, you can't come to the game! If it's little sister, tease her. If it's little brother, tell him what to do, and who wants small fry around?† And the same things can happen when there's no question of relationship, but when you come in contact with . . .

"Horrible Upper-Schoolers," Big Kids, and Teen-Agers

Older boys and girls push me around

I always have to do exactly as anybody older tells me to

Get ting sent to bed when others can stay up

G eting spanked for what my sesters do

The big Kids at school alwas pike on me

Getting picked on.

Getting in trouble with bigger kids.

Big kids boss you around.

Big kids, hit you, slap you, and always beat you.

I can't go along with some big kids.

---

†See page 9, "Where Did You Go? Out. What Did You Do? Nothing." by Robert Paul Smith (1957, New York, W. W. Norton & Company, Inc.). Just page 9? Nonsense! Read the whole book. Do it now.

dumb grownups
no responsibility
horrible upper-schoolers

Putting this chamber of horrors into tabulated form:

The big kids	always hit you
	bet up on me
	pick on you.
Bigger children	are always beating up on you.
Girls	are kicking boys in the shins.
Older children	Being teased by
	(14-18) call you a punk.
Older kids	acting like they can beat. you up all the time
	beat you up
	in High School push me around
	You get pick on by
	you pudhed a around by
Also older kids	say, "Get out of here, scram."
Other kids	bother you and call you names
	won't let me play kick ball or baseball
Other bigger kids	beat up on you
Some kids	call you names. and if you got bad eyes, they laugh
Teen-agers	do things we don't like
	people think their so big if their a teenager
	push you around
	teas you
	You get called a kid by, and they make you do all the work
	We get pushed around by

List the things that bother you most about ~~grown-ups~~ *teenagers*.

a) Sometimes they boss you around.

b) My brother always says my faults and everything to my friend

c) They say your gonna go somewhere special. Next day you don't go.

List three things you will always remember to do around children when you grow up.

a) Not to show off and hurt them just because I'm bigger,

b)

c)

List three things you promise you won't say or do to kids when you grow up.

a) Not to beat them up.

b) Not to Tell them stuff like: Who do you like better, your father or your mother. That gets them embarrassed

List three things which really trouble you about being a kid.

a) Your smaller and that makes some big guys thing their so great.

b)

You can be the wrong size; you can be the wrong age, too. "You're either too young or too old" is the burden of some 35 questionnaires in the "trouble" sub grouping. Among these we're treated to the other side of the "big brother, big sister" coin . . .

I'm too young to do things.
My little brother bugs me all the time.

I'm the oldest so I have to take care of my sisters

when you too young to do something, but too old to do something else
being a child
being half - child and half grow - up (from a boy halfway to 24)

I'm the oldest and always get blaned for my younger brothers and sisters wrongs

you have no command
you're considered too young to do this and that
Well everyone thinks you can't do things because you're to young they say
Your mother is overprotective
If you're a girl and you like a boy everyone teases you

they always say that your to young for such and such things
you always get hand me downs
When my little brother gets me in trouble I cant do anything about it

. . . and a Miss Right-in-the-Middle, her pencil racing across the sheet, scrawls forth:

Why do Parents baby the youngest baby the oldest but the middle one gets no attention
Your mother doesnt even let you pick out your own clothes
My father always screams at me but not the other two

Can't Do, Can't Go; Can't Have, Can't Get

GROWNUPS' RESTRICTION of children's general activity, wanderlust, and possession takes its lumps as a "trouble" in griping so similar to what we've read in the "bother" section that to quote extensively would become tedious. These underprivileged ones are in a small minority, insofar as the point is listed as the only trouble with being a child. But several aver they're fenced in on all sides, their spokesman being a boy, 10 . . .

you can't do what you want to do
you can't go where you want to go
you can't get what you want

Reviewing the forms as a whole, one gets the feeling that the boys and girls realize that such fencing-in isn't forever—that sooner or later they, too, can **get to do all the grown-up things I know I can do.** There are, however, certain despairing young ones siding with one respondent who, omitting sex, age, and grade data entirely, wrapped up childhood's real troubles in full (almost) capitals as follows:

YOU CAn'T DO ANYTHInG
YOU HAVE TO DO EVERYTHIG

Considering the many references in preceeding pages to the things that children don't like to do, there was bound to be a group registering discontent in terms of . . .

"Work troubles me"

WE CULLED 20 questionnaires collectively bemoaning how **you always have to do work** and **you have to do so much.** Then, even as Moses before Pharaoh, a boy, 11, lamenting: **"Your like a slave."** And worse, **"Your always bieng hit"** and **"Your always learning something."** (Such as how to make bricks without straw?) **Grownups sometimes sit while kids work** is another's *J'Accuse!*

Herewith, then, is a roundup of **"unfavorite things"** loathed in common by both sexes. The household chores group tallies up to a landslide majority.

I have to shovel all the snow!"

having to do dishes	**washing windows**
having to make my bed	**wash the car**
cleaning my own room	**you have to wash your face and hands**
having to dust the floor	**you have to take a bath every night**
They make me pick up	**I hate to comb my hair†**
mowing the lawn	**I don't like to tie my shoes†**
trimming the grass	**I don't like to get dressed up†**
weeding the garden	**I have to go to chour** (choir?)
pulling dandelions	**going to the store**
dump the garbage	**They make you take pills**
I have to clean out my rabbits cage	**to take medicine**

The reluctant rabbit-cage custodian, above, suffers also from grown-up-type reluctance in the form of **my mother won't let me have another dog.**

Occasionally a child's complaint about the work load states that **no one will help you do work,** and for parents who wonder why a child seems duller than he/she needs to be there's this admonition out of Fifth Grade:

Work to much. Don't get enough time to read.

"You have to eat icky food"

FOR MENU PLANNERS there follows a checklist of foods and non-alcoholic beverages named anywhere in the forms:

†" . . . for sunday school." Etc.

beans	snakes	
brussel sprouts	sower crute; saurkraut	
caulifloeer	spinach	pie
cows tongue		pizzas
eag plant	cake	pop; soda pop
eggs	candy	soda
fish on friday	coffee	sweets
gulosh	Coke	tea
liver (ick!)	hamburgers	

milk ("when you drink [it] they drink coffee")

orange juice ("they make you drink [it] at breakfast)

pepper	gum; bubble gum	
potatoes	ice cream	

. . . and surely no American household needs telling which of these foods the children consider to be most icky! Only one, a Sixth Grader, was bothered by grownups because **they make you eat slow and politely.** From responses to Question 4 and some "further comments" we hear . . .

I have to eat everything on my plate.

have to eat alot.

They neaver let me have a hanster.
I hate to eat my dinner.
I can't have very many sweets.

When you can not have dessert if you don't eat supper

I do not like to eat eag plant in which my mom and dad make me taste it al the time whem we have it. when my mom and dad have fights.

Eating food I don't like

You can't drink pop when ever you want it

We dont get desert
Our elders dont have to eat all thier supper but we do

I have to eat sower crute

You can't talk at the table.

You have to eat everything you got in your plate even if you don't like it.

They make me eat the vegetables I <u>hate</u>.

Eating food that grown ups like

You have to eat vegetables you don't like

You can't cook enough . . . I don't like some of the food at hot lunches

and your mother won't let you take cold lunch.

you have to mind.
you can't eat icecream or cake when you want.
you can't drink soda when you want to.

They wont Let us eat candy

can't buy lots of candy

. . . I would like to say that these things I wrote down are not made up I hate brussells sprouts

. . . and **brussell sprouts** and **brussel sprouts,** as on page nine. Two guidelines out of Question 1 ought to be helpful in the cause of peace at family tables:

They make you eat when you are not hungry.

They make me eat foods I've already tried and don't like.

. . . suggesting that it will be easier all around to let appetite and time shape young palates. Force-feeding? EE-uck!

Children's Fears

"I'M AFRAID!" "I'm scared!" Breathes there a grownup who can't bring to mind some times and conditions when he as a child knew apprehension and dread? What trepidations plague this new generation? Fewer than 10 percent of our group admits to "running scared" because of anything. Nevertheless, a number of young ones testify to more than just trouble over being a child. For the record, the anxious ones in Fifth Grade outnumber the other three grades combined. They say, the *girls* again identified by *italic* type . . .

Thinking about the future

you worry about what is going to happen later on

What will happen next to me

Growing up. Going to school. Thinking about the future.

Worrying about the future. My friend R.t.O. The teachers.

List three things which really trouble you about being a child.

a) _Being scared_

b) _lonelyness_

c) _doing things right_

Any further comments? _The school bothers me sometimes._
I am afraid the kids at school don't like me.
These things bother me all day and all night

Grade: _Five_   Your Age: _10_

I always get sent to my room for being bad
You wonder what will happen in the   future.

Future

will you fail or will you pass in school
will you be able to make a good living when you grow up

Geting shot.   Growing up.

when nobody will play with you   and you
When bigger people ask you somthing   Don't know.

I want to be 21 year's old . . . I do not want to go to war.†

When I do something wrong and I don't tell anyone
When I get bad marks and I have to have the paper signed
When I want something and I'm scared to ask for it

Not getting my   homework done
losing a book
not paying attention

Any further comments?   "No ? ? ? !"

Math. bieng sik.

If you get hurt, they say "It will be allright!"

your afraid you will die in the night

We get cold and my father almost never gets a cold.

when you get bad school marks or below 75.

Grownups always think that whatever you ⁄ think
No one trusts you.   doesn't count.
They think you have no   worries, but you do.

no money in the bank

Well some times school close
Some times someone well skear me
Someone well take tome when I am working

Ⓐ PEOPLE IN COLLAGE HAVE NOTHING TO WORRY AB-
OUT. Ⓑ WE HAVE LOTS

All the boys make pretend they have machine guns and shoot
at me because I was born in Germany. Every body calls me a tom
boy. . . . My mother says I'm a baby.

Dark places.   too much homework.

getting good grades in school
will I get through the summer without breaking an arm or leg

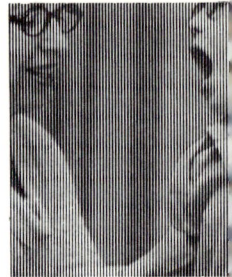

Falling out of trees. Getting cut. Staying back one year in school.
I get mixed up.

you   get   frighten easy. $\wedge$ a fraid of everything ^{you get}

Sometimes you get cheated because you don't understand the right price

I'm troubled about the darkness.
I'm troubled about my families, and my father.
I'm afraid of scary stories, When I get to bed, I can't go to sleep.

being weak. being Mien. bad graeds

being in a big crowd
being the only child at a party etc.

you think you'll never grow up

Having doctors trouble me
Dentists trouble me

For one Master or Miss Age 10 the trouble is **Growing up in a war fare nation**—and more (see page 61)—while another looks askance at **Positions of the world,** and hopes to *do* something about it . . . **Yes! I will try to make people congrecate and know how hard life is for negro's or poor people.** In all grades there's worry about **getting into trouble so much, get in to a lots of trouble, and I get in trouble all the time.** Sixth Graders say:

What will I do when I grow up
Will I do good in school

Wondering what will happen to me.
If I will be married or not.
If I will get a good job.

Not being able to help my country or family.

you have to face a different life later on
have to face things that happen to parents

That I might not pass in school   or not do good in my work.

Waiting to grow up
Wishing you never will grow up
Be ing confused

If I do something I shouldn't have done, I'm afraid to
tell my parents.

My mother thinks I don't like boys.
Our teacher is nice but ~~shee~~ not strict so I → don't get some assignments in on time and some, I don't even get in. So I'm worried about whats going to happen in Jr. High.

Being afraid of the dark.
Being afraid when left alone.
Afraid of dogs even at 12.

Well you're always looking in the future and you have to wait along time

What's going to happen to the world.

We wont get to see what happens in 100 years

I wonder what my future will be like.
I have many questions.
I sometimes wonder if I will loose all my friends.

Everybody laughs cos' I'n afraid of the dark

Getting good grades on my → *report card.*
I am so little that I wear a size → *between, a 8 and 10 and there isn't*
any 9.

Not being able   to   answer questions
worrying about   the   war.

Afraid of kidnapping.

In school I have a lot of trouble in arithmetic.
I don't like to read when we have to read by our selfes in school.
Any further comments? Every year I miss a lot of days in school and I'm so
poor in arithmetic that I'm afraid not to pass.

A Miss Age 11 very nicely prints: "I hope to live in a nice neighborhood
and have nice neighbors."

Over and above getting a licking, one Third Grader worries about getting
a harder licking, and missing the bus. Others claim get hert, getting very sick,
getting burned, and in to trouble. Similar Fourth Grade anxiety has been quoted on pages 51-52, 55-56. Triple trouble in the form of Problems. Household.
Worries plagued one boy, and from answers to Question 1 there are . . .

Sometimes their grouchy and scare you.   When their mad we're scared

Recall, from previous chapters, kids who are uneasy when They try to
show off. They go right on when there is a train stop. They drive to fast and
When they go out and don't come back till very late.

There is considerable dispirited comment about this matter of part-time
absentee parenthood, of which more later. Meanwhile, you can gauge the children's feelings from these typical declarations by older children:

Mom and Dad don't arn't home enough.
I don't get to see much of my mother and father.

Grown-ups always go out to eat and go to parties.

I can never go with my parents to parties.

My parents say you can not go to adult parties.

You can not do any thing with out your parents with you.

I hate being the baby of the → *family everyone worries about you.*

You never get your own way.

I alway get left home on saturdays → *while my parents go out and I*
always get left out of things.

you have to have a babby sitter

you can't go anywhere

you can't go out to eat with mom and Dad

On a more poignant note, ages nine and eight tell us . . .

Being a child hurts when you cry.

A child likes to go many places.

If I would never grow up, I would[n't] be somewhere in the world.

I don't like to be spanked with the wooden spoon

to be real dirty and to skip a bath

and to not be loved by my mom and dad

. . . but exasperation is the keynote—over being babied, bossed around, yelled at, pounded, patronized, ignored, deceived, delimited, disdained and disrespected, or just because . . .

"It's hard"

THIS SUMMING-UP by a Sixth Grader (page 77) is an excellent two-word description of the trouble with being a child.

It's hard **That I have to go to bed early!** It's hard **When we say something sometimes our parients don't listin!** It's hard because **You don't ever get to drive a car until your 16.**† It's hard because, says Miss Age 9 in Third Grade, **"You can't go on dates is still a long time. Then the one you see you might want but some one might get the one you want."** A classmate, male, sighs, **"Trying to make a friend (It is Hard)."**

In brief, it's hard to wait out the years when **it's always grownups' hour** seems to be the ordained state of the universe. It's dull, too, when . . .

People always help you when you want to do something by yourself
(It's too boring being a kid. I want to be a teenager)

Everybody always think your to young to do anything

I think it is boring to be a child

Nothing els troubles me

† " . . . but I do in Canada." A triumph for an Age 11 boy among the automotively deprived. For the record, approximately eight percent of the boys and girls named "can't drive" as a trouble, and a third of these put it at the top of the list.

Some final and good words on the subject of junior citizenship in a grown-ups infested world came from a Master Age 10, whose considered opinion was . . .

You can't do anything that's fun.
Have to do things that aren't any fun.
It's just no fun.

Any further comments? **Yes, I wish they would let you ride a bike on the streets.**

Young friend, perhaps you've had it better than you think. In my day, *they* wouldn't let *me* ride a bike on the sidewalk! — *Ed.*

CHAPTER VIII

" . . . AND SHINING MORNING FACE, CREEPING
LIKE A SNAIL UNWILLINGLY TO SCHOOL."

a) *The "story of my life" is school.*

b) *Everything you do has to be perfect.*

SCHOOL is a six-letter word occurring not as often as you might expect in this gathering of opinion—source, schoolchildren. It does appear in sufficient quantity to segregate (a nine-letter word *completely absent* from the children's responses) and ponder. It occurs most frequently in the answers to Question 4, hardly at all in answers to Question 1.

In sorting the questionnaires we tried to "think education" as well as "school," and watched therefore for papers with the subject named in such words as *teachers* and *homework*, or *arithmetic*, *gym*, *"inglish*," or other related language. Our final pile of school/education papers numbered a fifth of the total. We tried to determine which are troubled most by school, the boys or the girls. It appears to be the boys, in a ratio of six to five.

The phrase most often used by the youngsters is a simple, declarative **I have to go to school.** It seems not far-fetched to visualize this as uttered with the kind of resignation expressed by the word " SIGH " in a balloon over the head of *Peanuts'* Charlie Brown. A few samples from Fourth Grade speak for the lot:

> **school.**
> **You have to go to school.**
> **Going school.**
> **Going to school.**

we half to go to school.
You got to go to school.
Having to have to go to school.

. . . and so on into well over a hundred similar bald statements. For the rest of this chapter please bear in mind that they exist—as a vociferous unquoted majority, so to speak.

Remember our one from Third Grade bothered by **nothing, nothing, nothing** with respect to grownups, then who listed his/her troubles as **skoolol, mother,** and **father?** It should be noted in passing that skoolol is where he/she, when grown up, will remember to send his/her children. A few more from this level show some of the things, in brief, that children tie in with school as a real trouble about being a child. Answering Question 4 . . .

We can not saty up and whict t V
We have to go to school.
We have to do what the grow-up tell us.

Going to bed.
Git up in the morning.
I hate school.

hait them to go to scool
hait to have them die
hait to see them die

everybody boss me a round
we have to go go to school
we can not go babysitting

I always have to go to bed.
I hate school.

I have to go to school
I get the measles sometimes.
I don't like to go to bed at night.

When children do speak of school in Question 1, it's usually in terms of what grownups make you do about it. Here's a Third Grade form illustrating the distinction:

1. a) **They smoke.**   *4. a)* **school.**
   b) **They make you go to school.**   *b)* **being small.**
   c) **I don't get allowence.**   *c)* **getting spanked.**

Any further comments?   **I dont like school.**

In Fourth Grade the **we-half-to-go-to-school** dirge continues, with a few voices soloing now and again above the chant, among them one of our bored young people from last chapter: **Grownups can go places we have to go to school.** Another sings a short hymn in anti-praise of **Bible school, choir,** and **sometimes school.**

A 10-year-old girl (the one who complained that **I have to wait to get married**) tops even that trouble with **going to grade school.**

From Age 9: **I won't have to go to school when I'm big. Teacher makes me mad sometimes.**

From 9½: **School! You can't use your own money.**

From some Age 10s: **To go out. To stay up late. To be up in high school. They get to drive. You got to go to school.**

You are so small and there so big. You are so young and there so old. You have to go to school.

I hate school. I hate to eat. I hate snow.

Going to school so many days. They say no breaks when working.

Moving up into Fifth Grade, here's real, real, real trouble at age 10½ . . .

School
School
School

Any further comments? ~~me~~ **no sir!**

You always have to ask to go somewhere.
If you fool in the house you get H a n g.
You have to go to awful school.

This is another girl, 10, unburdening herself. From an Age 12, he or she . . .

Nothing troubles me about being a child except going to school.

Again it could be a boy or girl protesting as follows:

Can't go out. Don't like school.

Any further comments? **Why do we have to go to school ? ? ? ? ? ? ? ? ?**

> You can never go to dance's
> You can never drive a car
> You have to go to school

Any further comments? **Why do we have to go to school?**
Please answer my questions. Why can't we drive a car.

Two girls vary the standard complaint with **Having so many years of school** and **If you don't get strait A's you have to go to summer school.** From another young lady of 10 . . .

> **Why we hardly ever get priviles?**
> **" " " " about always get yelled at?**
> **" " do we have so many school?**

Any further comments? **How come in school some kids are more popular than others I don think it's fair.**

A 12-year-old's . . .

> **th e h om e work**
> **always the ~~under~~ underdog**
> **always ge t kicked out of classes at sch ool**

. . . graduates us from Fifth to Sixth Grade, where one Age 11 bothered by grownups because **We have to go to school** drives the point home as his No. 1 trouble by specifying **You have to go to school Monday to Friday.** Yes, **"you got to go through a lot of school"** and **"you have to go to school for 12 years,"** echo two more Age 11s, while a temperature-sensitive twelve-year-old comments, **"I don't like going to school on cold days."** For another, the trouble is that **school last to long!** A boy, 12, avers . . . **7 hours a day**

> **I don't like to not be able to work**
> **I don't like to have to attend school**
> **I don't get to go to some movies**

. . . and another, whom we visualize as a boy in one of those sudden spurts in which he outgrows all his clothes and accouterments, winds up a briefly worded questionnaire observing that . . .

> **the school desk aren't vary good.**

Reverting to Fifth Grade for a moment, we wondered about one child's **Going to go a different schools.** (Followed by ? ? ?) Was he or she worried about attending Sixth Grade in a different school building, or was this a victim of a family's moving from community to community, perhaps propelled by an employer's decisions on where Dad should work?

Fifth Grade, from which we received the largest number of school oriented responses, yielded some visually high-impact questionnaires.

4.a) **when you are the oldest**
  b) **have to tead to a bady**
  c) **and   H A V E   S C H O O L.**

4.a) **N O T H I N G   B u g s   M e**
  b) **I   just   want   to   get   out   of   school**
  c)

. . . and this one, an Age 10, had also lettered **I'm H A P P Y** in billboard-size print, a light green color, on the *reverse* of the sheet.

To some of the boys and girls school is just another manifestation of grownupism spelled t-e-a-c-h-e-r. However, of our school group of questionnaires, only a tenth focuses on the teacher-type adult. In relation to the whole body of questionnaires this is a drop in the bucket, although it is likely that many boys and girls are including teachers when they speak of grownups in terms of "they." From a school where a trace of don't-spare-the-rod yet lingers in its method, we have . . .

List the things that bother you most about grownups. (teack~ers~)

> **They don't let you by a new bike**
> **They boss yow a round**
> **They don't let yow turn off the lights**

List three (things) you will always remember to do around children when you grow up.

> **Take em to movies**

List three things ~Youxproxkast~ you won't say or do to kids when you grow up.

> **I not**

List three things that really trouble you about being a child.

> **T E A C H E R S**
> **C A N' T MAKE R ULES**
> **CAN'T MAKE NOI S E**

Any further comments?   **Teacher spank hard, I think**
Are you a boy? **I think So**   *Your grade: Your age:*   **11½**

Bothered by grownups because of **teachers, air force,** and **moving away from everybody** (and troubled as a child by **work, teachers,** and **I cann't do what I want**) is a Fifth Grade boy of 12. The following miscellany on teachers is from children's answers to Question 1:

> **Like your teacher made you write 100 times I will not talk**
> **Other school teacher given you the board of**
> **I don't like going to school.**
> **I don't like the teacher's.**
> **My teacher makes us write a lot.**

the teacher makes use do home work

Have trouble with teachers

Teachers get mad over every little thing

The way teachers boss you around

Our teacher makes use stay after s^{kh}ool.

. . . not to mention one already quoted on page 34. Continuing, with responses again from Question 4:

1. In school I don't like to answer questions because the teacher scolds me for answering her or him a senseless question. 2. The teacher never lets you to consult with other pupils.

when the teacher always gets mad and you didn't really do it.

Compare form above with "Age 11½" quoted on page preceding. We guess that these two sit across the aisle from each other. But note the differences, too.

List the things that bother you most about grown-ups.

a) ~~The Techer She~~ _She gives to much_

b) _english_

c) _____

List three things you will always remember to do around children when you grow up.

a) _keep the kids happy_

b) _____

c) _____

List three things you promise you won't say or do to kids when you grow up.

a) _I won't whip I ~~will~~ will do it_

b) _some other way._

c) _I won't cuse_

List three things that really trouble you about being a child.

a) _school_

b) _Can't make rules_

c) _____

Any further comments? _____

_____

_____

_____

Your Town: _____ Your School: _____ Your ____ e: _5_ Your Age: _10_
Are you a boy? _✓✓✓_ Or Girl? _____

you get hit
you firght
    and your principal don't ter you righ

If, as a Sixth Grade young lady says, **"Some teachers don't understand Kids,"** sometimes the kids have trouble understanding teachers:

Well the teachers don't listen to your side of the story

at school you can't say ain't. or you have to write a sentence a hunder times. They make the hole class stay in for talking when it is only one or two people talking in the room.

Teachers act so mean but when mothers come to visit they act so nice. Teachers cheak someone else's but not yours!

I wish Parents and teachers would relise we aren't babies any more!

111

**techer bug me more than any one and I do not like her I bug her
I think**

**Everyone expects me to do 9th grade work.
My teachers won't let me read mystery books.**†

It is **especillay teachers,** claims a boy, 12, in Sixth Grade, who are the grownups who pick on kids a lot. **Teachers always nagging** and **people and teachers at school they are to strick** occur to remind adults of some aspects of classroom atmosphere they may have forgotten.

Lest the educators feel that they are being singled out, either editorially or by the children, as a target for this book, here are some responses for them to show to their school boards. First is an Age 11, Fifth Grade, taking a dim view of grownups as "They" in his answer to Question 1:

**They Hate us
They Punish us
They don't let us do what we want to do**

... but what troubles him/her about being a child is only **Teacher** (but not all)
                                                                                                   rules
                                                                                                   money

Then here's an Age 9 whom grownups bother because . . .

**They make you do work.
They have more fun than we do.
They can be a teacher and we can't.**

Perhaps this Third Grade master or miss envies teacher status under the impression that teachers are blissfully free from school work, for he/she goes on to name the troubles about being a child as: **You can not have any fun. You have to do school work. You have to go to bed early.** (How early do teachers go to bed when they have papers to mark?) Another expression of longing from same grade, same age, female: **I wish I were out of schol. I wish I were a teacher.** (Return to page 5 to read something else she longs to be!)

While on the subject (of t-e-a-c-h-e-r), are there any further comments?

Any further comments?　　　　**Yes, When I get older I'm going to be
very good to children, and if I'm going to be a teacher I won't
hurt anyones feelings.**

Any further comments?　　　　**I like all the teacher, except when one
hits me then I realy could hit them right back . I like
Mr. G----- most of the time and Mrs. D--- and Mrs. E--------Mrs. D-------
and Mrs. H------------**

†And she promises: "I won't expect them to read 'background' books."

List the things that bother you most about grown-ups.

a) _If you get angry if you get a B then you point out_
b) _make you clean your room EVERY DAY_
c) _____

List three things you will always remember to do around children when you grow up.

a) _____
b) _____
c) _____

List three things you promise you won't say or do to kids when you grow up.

a) _will not tell them to clean their room everyday_
b) _____
c) _____

List three things which really trouble you about being a child.

a) _getting good marks_
b) _trying to do what grownups want you to do_
c) _just being good_

Any further comments? _grownups are IMPOSTIBLE_
you try to please them and they get ugly say
angry

Your School: _____ Your Grade: _5_ Your Age: _11_

List the things that bother you most about grown-ups.

a) _They can go out dancing._
b) _They can boss us around._
c) _They can go to bed late at night._

List three things you will always remember to do around children when you grow up.

a) _Be nice to them._
b) _Say nice things to them._
c) _____

List three things you promise you won't say or do to kids when you grow up.

a) _Hurt them badly._
b) _Not to scare them out of there wittis._
c) _Not to teach them to sware._

List three things which really trouble you about being a child.

a) _You have to do what the teacher tells you._
b) _You have to do your homework or stay in for recess_
c) _You have to go to school._

Any further comments? _Yes one, do you like being a_
grown up? why
_____

Your Grade: _5_ Your Age: _11_

Another Age 9, whom we guess to be a girl from her use of the feminine pronoun, writes that what she will always remember to do around children is:

let her stay after school and help her teacher.

Then we have a Fourth Grade Age 9 resentful of grownups' swearing, smoking, meanness, and cruelty. He/she is troubled by **older children think they're smart and push me around** and by **getting in trouble when I don't do wrong,** but gives two cheers for grownups with . . .

Any further comments?   **My parents aren't half as bad as some and parents know better than we. My teacher is a good one, and is a very nice person**

Finally, from the same age and education level, a girl we've quoted before (in another context) and would like to quote again, in full this time, and not only because of her pro-teacher proclivity. Do you hear and see yourself in this one? . . .

1.a) **Mommy always says that a certain thing would be good for dolls,** in front of my friends, and I stopped years ago.
  b) **Or she says, "My — you look like you havn't brushed your hair."**
  c) **Sometimes "9 years old. It seems like yesterday when you were 6¾"**

2.a) **To be funny, or serious, and try to make them like me.**
  b) **Make sure they don't get out of hand.**   children.
  c) **If both grown-ups and children are around, try to amuse** ↗

3.a) **I won't be too lazy, and I will not tease (too much)**
  b) **I won't say, "shut-up" or "You bother me."**
  c) **I won't say, "How cute you are" or, "My, your not at all growing"**

4.a) **Grown-ups always get their own way.**
  b) **Mommy makes me go to bed early.**
  c) **Mommy says that I have to go on a diet.**

Any further comments?   **Yes!**
  I would like to be a Teacher when I grow up. I want to be a teacher for 4th grade. I hope to give out things like this.

"We get a lot of homework from school"

SOMEWHAT LESS than 10 per cent of the "school" questionnaires bring up the subject named by the boy quoted above, a ten-year-old in Fifth Grade, even if we stretch the term as described earlier in this chapter. There is, of course, the lively clutch of forms pointing out that grownups make children "work and work"—at doing the dishes, housecleaning, errands, chores, often in a tone of voice implying that if grownups are so smart, why weren't these

List the things that bother you most about grown-ups.

a) They say they'll get you something and then they always "don't"

b) They always say they have no money when you ask for something

c) They break promises - like they say your — (Back)

D) They make kids do all the work and →

List three things you will always remember to do around children when you grow up.

a) Try to help —

b) Listen to what they say. (for once)

c) Let them play anything they want.

List three things you promise you won't say or do to kids when you grow up.

a) I won't say, "You can't do this or that even →

b) I won't swear around my kids.

c) I won't smoke or drink around my →→

List three things that really trouble you about being a child.

a) Nobody listens to me. →

b) Make me eat junk I don't

c) I have to study during my favorite T.V. show

Any further comments? Teachers say "You can come up for help any time," so when you do, they say, "What? You don't know this??" And they give you the full treatment

Your Grade: 6 Your Age: 12
Or Girl? YES

things abolished long ago? Some of the kids gripe about both, and for a few there's not only work, but worry, as in this Fourth Grade, Age 10, example in response to Question 4:

> **School because I'm worried that I don't get my work done**
> **I am worried that when I get home there be dishes**
> **That one of these days I won't like to work.**

115

1. 'but they always have enough for something for them.

2. friend can come down and at the last minute they say "No, I'm too busy today." EEUCK!

4. they just lie around,

3. if your friend's mother lets he do it.'

4. kids.

5. like,

6.

In answers to Question 1. a) we find **my mother doesn't help me on my homework** and a girl's **when my brothers and sister bother me at homework.** A boy, 11, gives grownups the needle with . . .

They forget their school lessons just when you need help with your homework.

And a girl, 12, chimes in . . .

They are two old fashoin.

They don't understand our new ways of doing school work.

In responses to Questions 2 and 3, some forward-looking ones promise:

I'll help them with their school work

I'll help them with school projects

I will not bug them about their homework

I will help them with homewoke

I will not send them to bed if they don't have their homework done

. . . but the homework subject, like school itself, predominates in responses to Question 4. The first quotation, at left, is an Age 11, boy, speaking:

School	**is being a 9 year old girl**
home work	**I dom't like school**
and home and school responsibility	**is doing wark at school**

The teacher makes you do a lot of work

You have to go to school I like some work in school but Some I hate

For some, homework itself seems not so much the anathema as various problems associated with it:

When they make you come inside at 4:00 to Do your homework

when I come home I got to work & work satday I got towork to 4:00 clock I got to clean of the hous

Well you have to wate to you birthday You have to wite when you get out of school And you have to do wrok.

"I an a girl," whispers a penciled tracery at the bottom of this questionnaire. At the top is her name and address, complete with zip code. A tentative correspondent for Miss Lonelyhearts? With all sympathy for an impatient Miss Age 11 in Sixth Grade, we interpret this as a bid for release from the three Ws — **wate**ing, **wite**ing, and **wrok**.

Continuing the homework and other problems exploration . . .

Why they make you do your homework right when you get home

Getting home work and can't watch t. v.

Is it o k for a parent to help with homework?

answer these questions:

List the things that bother you most about grown-ups.

a) _THEY BRAG ALOT_

b) _THEY TALK SO YOU CAN HEAR WHAT THER_

c) _SAYING AND MAKE you DO JOBS._

List three things you will always remember to do around children when you
grow up.

a) _I WILL REMEMBER NOT TO BRIBE CHILDREN_

b) _I WILL REMEMBER NOT TO LET THEM SAY WRON_

c) _I WILL REMEMBER TO LET THEM DO_
THEIR OWN THINKING.

List three things you promise you won't say or do to kids when you grow

a) _I WON'T GET MAD AT THEM ALOT._

b) _I WON'T TELL THEM LIES._

c) _I WON'T BRIBE THEM._

List three things that really trouble you about being a child.

a) _I CAN'T DO WHAT I WANT TO DO!_

b) _I CAN'T. DRIVE A CAR._

c) _I DON'T GET ANY MONEY TO SPEND!!_

Any further comments? _YES!!!!! I think that_
you SHOULDN'T HAVE TO HAVE A
COLLEGE EDUCATION TO GET A GOOD JOB.

Your Town:_____ Your School:_____ Your Grade: _6_ Your Age: _1_
Are you a boy? _X_   Or Girl?___

*Could this boy have heard about the many distinguished school dropouts who
nevertheless "made good" when they grew up?*

118

List the things that bother you most about grown-ups.

a) *When they say good things about you to the teacher.*
b) *They always talk about your goods side (when they are not true)*
c) *Your grandmothers talk about how pretty you are.*

List three things you will always remember to do around children when you grow up.

a) *Show them how to do the dishes*
b) *Show them how to wax the floor.*
c) *When they get grown-up they can relax from doing those stupid things.*

List three things you promise you won't say or do to kids when you grow up.

a) *I won't spank them unless I have to.*
b) *I'll try not to embarrass them.*
c) *I'll let them go swimming and to the movies when they want to.*

List three things which really trouble you about being a child.

a) *You always have to ask to go somewhere.*
b) *If you fool in the house you get Hang.*
c) *You have to go to auful school.*

Any further comments? *Yes, It's terrible to be a kid. (rather be a grown-up and not get embarrassed)*

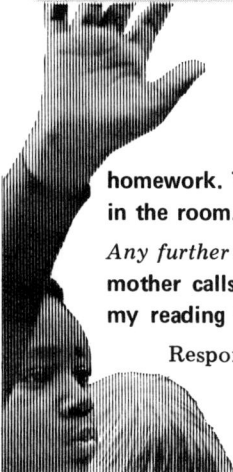

Gee! they hardly buy any clothes for you and never let you play when you have homework

They tell you to read to your brother when you have homework. To do your homework but let your brother and sister in the room.

Any further comments? yes, for example when I'm reading my mother calls me to a dozen chores and then I won't get back to my reading for hours.

Responses from two Age 11s pair off on the subject:

Have to work	school
Have to go to school	can't drive
	can't work

. . . presenting work on the one hand as a condition of existence along with school, on the other hand as something a young lady numbers among those restrictions grownups are always imposing. Could it be a groovy job, for money, or just because, as another anti-schooler complains, **"You can't have big, fat wallets"** —work or no work? From two Age 10s in Fifth Grade . . .

> **You have to do the dirty work**
> **You get no pay at school when you do work**
> **On Saturday there is no school but all we do is work.**

. . . and from an Age 11 (still in Third Grade) we hear:

> **I do not like to work.**
> **I do not like school.**
> **I do not like school work.**

A boy, 12, analyzes the situation in a thoughtful postscript. Untroubled by having to go to school, he is one of the ones who wants to make his own decisions, be allowed to **do things within reason,** and have the right to vote:

> *Any further comments?* **I think that teachers and parents give you to much work and expect you to get it done in a short period of time.**

Amen! Now is there something else about school that troubles children? Take it from one who said (as have so many before him), **"The best thing about school is recess."** For him as for others school is that place **you have to go to,** and when you get there . . .

"YOU HAVE TO DO ARITHMETIC"

ON THIS MATTER the forms tell us little of whether there is a boy or girl majority, so let's just listen to the chorus, in which all ages are represented:

> **Always having to go to school and doing arithmetic.**
> **Doing arithmetic.**
> **You at to go to school. You at to do arithmetic.**
> **arithmetic bothers me.**
> **to do my arithmetic.**
> **Not to arithmetic.**
> **I don't like arithmetic.**
> **I hate arithmetic.**
> **I hate arithmetic in School.**
> **I don't like to do arithmetic.**
> **Arithmetic bother's me and**
> **I'm so afraid at the end of the school year that I'm not going to pass.**

And a spirited coda for the four-letter version . . . **Math.**
Some of the problems we have in math.
You can't do math hardy.
Learn Math.
I haet math.
I Don't like doing the New Math. Or doing the dishes.

There you have it, math teachers—a rating with dishwashing on the scale of juvenile anathema. But take comfort; berated by only 19/250ths of the kids who take umbrage at school anyway, your subject preoccupies a wee fraction (0.0154975) of our thousand-plus boys and girls. Moreover, not another subject except reading gets any such accolade as the one that follows, written with a flourish and decorated with a pencil sketch of the symbol of the flower people:

Any further comments? **I like being a child because you can go to carnival and all kinds of things. You can go to school too. I like math best in school.**

The source is a boy or girl in Fourth Grade, and there is a gung ho arithmetician in Third Grade, too, a girl, 9, who said . . .

Whell I like [name of school] **I like to go to school to learn times table.**

Transiting out of math into reading is easy because two members of the arithmetic chorus, above, have rough words for that, too: **Have hard work. Hard books to read.** and **You at to do raeding.** An Age 11, he or she, is both bothered and troubled because . . .

1.a) **I dont like my mother tell people that I cant read good.**

b) **I dont like mom to tell people that I have trouble in my arithmetic.**

4.a) **I dont like my school.**

b) **I wish I had more help in reading.**

Concerning reading, the consensus is that it's the least troubling of school subjects, yet how pitifully few reports there are to glean a consensus from! Troubles *a)*, *b)* of an Age 10 are **You don't go out as often** and **You don't get to read good books that are older.** A Miss Age 11 signs off her form with . . .

Any further comments? **I like or love to read and my parents won't let me. I won't to practice my piano only half hour and my parents make me practice an hour.**

Practice. She can say that again! In how many American homes is the battle joined over exactly how many hours, minutes, and seconds are to be spent struggling with keyboard and other instruments? Parenthetically, as a part of Education, Homework Division, we quote some responses from young ones who are bothered most about grownups because . . .

When ever I'm going to go outside she make me practice.

When they say to practice piano every day.

They make you practice plaing the oargan

My mom make me practice the piano forty minutes a day.

You may remember from the chapter on Third Grade that there was an Age 8 mourning that **I never can play the piano** or **laugh in the car.** This is *really* swimming upstream against the current of **remembering about practiceing my flute** and similar remarks. **My trumpet lesson** troubles a Fourth Grade boy, 10, even more than **school** and **grown-ups,** in the order named, and **I'll never make them study music** is the promise of another Age 10, male, in Fifth Grade.

The forgetful flautist just quoted is she who lambasted the New Math and dishwashing, which brings us back to the school curriculum again.

"**I have to learn history,**" says Miss Lisa, her grade and age omitted. A boy, 10, states in a growly kind of handwriting . . .

~~Tehe~~ ~~Teehor~~ ~~Ohne~~ **She gives to much englis h**

Physical Education rates three responses—two "troubles" and a "further comment," from Grades Three, Four, and Five. They are: **gym** . . . **Gym in school (Sort-of bothers me.) . . . I wish very much that our school could have a gym.**

Suddenly—lo!—on a Fifth Grade, Age 11, questionnaire so lightly penciled as to verge on the invisible, this lonely and stark admission . . .

Spelling is my toule

A Smattering of Appreciation

THERE ARE but a handful of questionnaires left that talk about school, all but one of them from Fifth and Sixth Grades. Adult rules and attitudes get a going-over in a small batch of answers to Question 1:

they wont let yow bring things to school so that yow wouldn't have to go out of your way to get them

When they visit shool and pat you on the head or something like that

I have to obey rules at school and at home

They always embarrass **you** **like if do something good in school and then they tell.**

Mr. J. yelling at the class

When they slap me — and not to bring gum to school.

They say you have it easy in school when we don't

And now hear these! Both are by Age 11s in Sixth Grade:

TEAchER iN bAd temper
TEAchER who stAys with book
BEiNg yEllEd At foR doing Nothing

The whole class being blamed for what a few people do.
Being balled out in front of everyone else.
Not being called on when you raise your hand, but the people who don't raise their hands get called on.

Any further comments?   I think   [name of school]   needs more discipline. Kids can get away with murder.

There is a smattering of appreciation of school values in some of the children's promises and resolves, when they grow up, to . . .

Tell them to go as far as they can in school.

make kids finish school

Never let them go without an education through college.

Make them earn their money except for school and thing like that

. . . although there is one back-handed compliment given as answer to Question 4: I hate school, but if I had a chanch to stay home, I wouldn't because I need the education.

It seems too bad that there aren't more who say . . .

I like school because I think I can get a better job with a good education

I like being in school. And I like the vice princala

. . . which last is from a Third Grade he or she. A boy, 10½, gives a cheer for school in reverse; he is really troubled about being a child because of **having to stop school in summer.** Parents and teachers of school-troubled young ones might well ponder the viewpoint of an Age 11 who, when he or she filled out the questionnaire, had virtually completed the primary grades (with honor, we trust) and would get next year's schooling in Junior High:

1.a) **If they tell you to do something you have to do it**
  b) **They put you on the spot a lot**
  c) **If they do something wrong it's "alright." Everything you do has to be perfect (they don't practice what they preach)**
4.a) **The "story of my life" is school**
  b) **Everything you do has to be perfect.**
  c)

Any further comments?   **No! Sorry**

THUS, fifty years and three centuries after Shakespeare, his "unwillingly to school" still says it for a lot of kids (remember the hundred and more **I got to go to school** lines we *haven't* quoted, not to mention the children's concern over achievement, as on pages 100-102). Must this joylessness in schooling persist? Why not more ferment, pro or con? Why so few comments on teachers and the curriculum, and nothing about projects, programs, experiments, and that peachy educational gadgetry called "hardware" by its buyers and sellers? Observe the children's own "grading," by omission, of things like: audio-visual instruction, zero; teaching machines, zero; band, zero; the laboratory sciences, zero (and demerits for math); assembly, zero; sex education, zero; guidance, zero; social studies (except for an enigmatic comment on history), zero; books and reading, next door to zero. So much about how school *troubles;* so little about what school *does.* How real the trouble with being a child if it's only...

School (Kinda)

... but, says a Sixth Grader, **"You have to do so much to have a good education."** Do *what? How* much? *How* good? Just scuttlebutt, or is it mutiny, Admiral?†

If we seem to harp on the matter editorially, it's because one of us, having had three children complete grade school, remembers that what bothered him most about the process was the almost total absence of feedback? What he wanted to know was—and is—what's happening in the classroom?* Why do not children once in a while come home from school eager and willing—and even able—to tell about it?

†"American Education—A National Failure" by H. G. Rickover. 1963, New York, E. P. Dutton & Co., Inc.

*For "a side to school the public never sees," look into page 116 of "What's Happened to Teacher?" by Myron Brenton. 1970, New York, Coward McCann, Inc. Illuminating also on subjects ranging from why children don't like math to textbooks that turn them off, from PTA to why teachers strike.

CHAPTER IX

EARLY TO BED AND EARLY TO RISE

The TV Generation

We are humens too, so we ought to be able to stay up late.

ONE OF US, having suffered the inhumanity of imposed (and enforced) bedtimes until he was darn near into college, was drawn with magnetic compulsion to questionnaires from children who had likewise tasted the bitter cup: **They make us go to bed early. Or, I can't stay up late. Or, They can stay up late and we can't.** He was chagrined when, after isolating and counting such questionnaires, there weren't enough to make a big to-do about it.

However, since the days when the Senior Editor lay fuming abed, his psyche badly bent by the injustice of it all, a thing called television has come to stay. As usual, the more gee-whiz miraculous our grown-up existence becomes, the more opportunity for grownups to say "NO" to kids. So that today's ('scuse please, *tonight's)* early-to-bed syndrome often enlarges to: **I can't stay up late and watch TV.**

What the children say about it contributes only obliquely to the to-do about TV's *influence* on them. Even the eldest—the handful of 13s and 14s present—have never lived in a world *without* television. Yet all are too young to have been day-in-day-out entertained by *Howdy Doody* or *Kukla, Fran and Ollie.* In the chronology of educational programming for children they're between *Ding Dong School* and *Sesame Street.*

To have some idea of the relative importance of TV in children's lives, we range through all sections of the forms and quote so that TV is allotted its proper *a)*, *b)*, or *c)* position. Remember that answers to Questions 2 and 3 are future tense: What they'll remember and/or promise to do when they grow up and have kids of their own. So that the **TV-bedtime** combinations stand out, we print them in **boldface**. *Italic* type identifies questionnaires we know to be from *girls*.

1....... **They put you to bed erly.**
They make you go to the store.
They make you tran the t.v. of

2....... Be very good to them.
Don't make them cry.
rock them to sleep.

3....... Not to hit them.
Not to kik.
Not to be ugly to them.

4....... here to much noies.
have to eat alot.
put you to bed erly.

Any further comments? No   *[Grade 3—Age 8]*

1....... **They won't let you w acth t.v.**
They boss you around.
They alwas spank you for nothing.

2....... Be nice to them.
Not make them work very much.
Let them eat whatever they want.

3....... I will not Be mean to them.
I won't make them go to bed to early.
I won't say do the dishes and make your bed.

4....... Every one bosses you around.
You have to go to school.
You never have fun.

Any further comments?   My Dad has a big mouth.
And my mom always tells me what to do.   *[3—8]*

1....... grown-ups hit us when we are bad.
grown - ups do not let us saty up.
they have to which were T V.

2....... **To put them in bed when its time.**
To give them a bate on satterdays.
To let them wich T V but not to late.

3....... Not to hit them.
Do this Do that.

st the things that bother you most about grown-ups.

When they smoke

When they hollar at you

When their false teeth fell out (not my parents)

e three things you will always remember to do around children when you
w up.

be nice to them

be intrested in what they do

dont hit them or embarrass them

t three things you promise you won't say or do to kids when you grow up

hit them

scold them

embarrass them

t three things that really trouble you about being a child.

you have to mind

you can't eat icecream or cake when you want

you can't drink soda when you want to

further comments? *they punish you if you*
bring a bad report card home

r Town:_____ Your School:_____ Your Grade: *5* Your age *11*
you a boy? ✔

The questionnaire above would seem to have little bearing on the matter at hand, but . . . . .

Not to make them work to hard.
4.......We can not saty up and whict t V.
We have to go to school.
We have to do what the grow-up tell us.   [3—9]

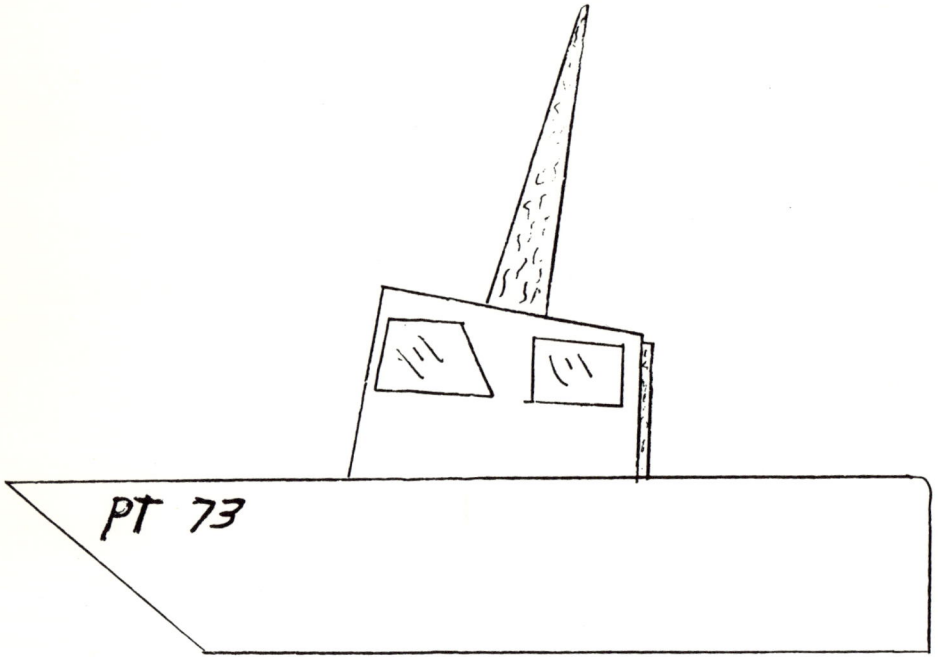

PT 73

.... *the drawing on back, of the flagship of* McHale's Navy, *is the most space any young viewer gave to a specific television program.*

1.......Macking me eat stufe I do not like.

My Brother bens my thume.

They make me leve my tv progrom sometimes.

2.......when they are hungry biy them some- theing to eat.   geve them snacks.

lete them stay up saterday night
3....... talk nastey.
    E a t snakes in front of them.
    hete them.
4....... every body pikes on me.
    they throw snow bolls ate me.
    I which I cou'd stay up later.   [3—10]

1....... they boss us around
    they command the T.V.
    and make you go to bed early
2....... be nice to them
    don't fight with them
    sometimes I will play games with them
3....... I won't say any bad worlds to kids.
    I won't be like a bully to them
4....... We get bossed around
    We get pushed around by teenagers   [5—10]

1....... When I get in trouble my mom tells everyone
    My mom always asks me what I've been doing when I
    She always gets mad when I do work in front of T.V. c̦ o
2....... When I grow I'm going to be real nice to my child.   me
    I going to take my children on trips all the time.   in.
3....... I won't tell my kids how to run their lives.
    I won't tell them who to marry.
4....... I don't think all kid is so bad.
    You alkways get bosed around.
Any further comments?   I don't think being a kid is so bad but
    the parents really get me.   [5—?]

1....... they boss you around too much
    don't let you stay up when there is a good show on
    don't let you play out in dark
2....... take a bath a lot   eat well   read a lot
3....... won't swear
    won't
    ʌ get everything they want
    won't
    ʌ **go to bed late**
4....... if you have a big brother he starts fights
    can't go someplace on school night!
    can't stay up at nights on weekends
                                                  [5—10]

1....... **They let you watch TV to much.**
2....... Watch (~~them~~) the children carfully.
small. Don't let (~~them~~) the children smoke when their
~~Take go~~ Take good care of them.
3....... I want hit or bet them.
When there small wont let them go out alone.
4....... Can't do the things grown ups can.   [5—12]

1....... They always want things perfect.
Pinch your cheek.
**Make you set the table when you're
trying to get your home work finished so you can watch
your favorite TV show later on.**
2....... Not make them eat everything on thier plate.
Put them to bed early.
Not to be old fashioned, keep up with new styles, etc.
3....... Sware in front of "the little ones"
Put them to bed early.
4....... If you are older, as I am, you have to do so many
chores around the house.   [6—11]

1....... When they tell people my nickname
When you can't watch a special show on T.V.
and then yell at you.   When their in a grouchy mood
2....... Help them learn the things that they
should and shouldn't do, and the things
that are hard in school.
3....... If they don't like their nickname I won't
tell people. **I will let them watch a
T. V. show if it doesn't go to late.**
4....... I am small and everyone critisizes me.
I'll try not to yell at kids when I grow up.   [6—12]

1....... Makeing us go to school
they don't give us enough money
they don't let us stay up and wach the late late show.
2....... let them do any thing
they want
be nice
3....... tell lies
cus
4....... You don't get to go to places that grownups
Any further comments?   Only that I wish that   [6—12]

1....... **When they don't let you stay up for good m**o*v*_i*e*_s

When they say to practice piano every day.

When you can't go out after supper.

*2.......Take care of them and keep them out of da*n*g*_e_r

Have fun and go on trips with them.

*3.......Not to be gone all day and leave them beh*_i_n_d

Favor ^{only} *one of the children.*

Not to be mean and say unkind things to ^{them}

4.......Nothing really troubles me of being a

child, everyone sometime is a child in ones life. [6—12]

1.......They get mad when their're worried.

They won't let me watch T. V.

They won't let pets sleep with one.

2.......Don't tell secrets around or by them.

I won't scold my child in front of his guest.

I won't yell for my child to come in.

3.......I won't be lax in my dicipline.

I won't buy all my child's clothing.

I won't let them watch T. V. all day.

4.......Not much freedom.

Being embassaseid by younger sisters.

Being pushed around too fast [6—12]

Time for a station break, so to speak. The questionnaires above, and others quoted elsewhere,† are all in which TV is either named or implied in a response to Question 1. For the rest, abridgment of the questionnaires (in a space-saving format as needed) won't spoil the story.

*2.......*I will never swear. **I will let them watch T.V. if thir good.** I will prise them for good paper.

*3.......*I will never hit them hard. I will never shot away. **I will never send them to bed and less they used bad manners.**

*4.......***You have to go to bed eraly.** You get pushed around. You don't get to talke. [3—8]

*2.......*Not talk about politics. Be nice to them. **If they want to watch T.V. I'll let them.** [5—10]

2....... **Let them watch t.V on week– nights.** Let them go to the beach alone.

*3.......***You can't watch t.v.** [5—11]

†Pages 14, 15, 29, 30, 31, 41, 44, 93, 106, 115, 117.

2.......Not to be mean. **Let them watch something if its very good ➔ no matter how late.** Let them say what they want.

3.......Hit them after 6 years old. Not let them play with other children. **Not let them watch t.v.**

4.......**I can't stay up as late as I want.** I can't talk back to adult. I can't boss them.

Any further comments? Adults please try to be better.   *[5—11]*

2.......Don't smoke! Give them pie when you eat it. **Not let them watch T.V. too much.**

2.......I won't tell them that they have grown. **I will let them watch what they want to on T.V.**

3.......I will not make them eat cows tongue. I won't yell at them for nothing at all.

4.......**I have to go to bed at 8:30**

3.......smake. wash mouth out. **and trun off tv when they are watching it.**

4.......**going to bed. when we are watching tv they come in and switch chanal.**   *[5—10]*

3.......*I will not fight with my husband.* **I will not let them watch T.V. if they fight.** *I will not yell at them only if there mean.*   *[3—8]*

3.......**Don't make them go without T V.** Don't tell them they can't go play. Don't say naughty words in front of them.   *[4—10]*

3.......Yell at them. Giving them a whoping. **Turn off TV.**   *[5—10]*

3.......**Say that when I was your age I used to do these** back side **and that insted of watching T.V.**   *[6—12]*

Another station break—to tune out "channels" 2 and 3. The following is exclusively in reply to Question 4, with further comments as identified:

4.......Always having to hurry up. **Somtimes I can't watch television.** I always have to go out and play.   *[4—9½]*

4.......Sometimes grownups always say were to young to do something. **My mom doesn't let me watch some shows.**   *[4—10]*

4.......You can't talk back. ~~You~~ **I can't whach t.v.** Don't go places.   *[5—10]*

4.......**Being sent to bed when other people stay up.** Being hit by my sister. **Getting home work and can't watch t.v.**   *[5—11]*

4.......**You don't get to stay up late. and you don't get to watch your own shows. and you can't go to stores at 9:00** *like they sometimes do.* [5—10]

4.......you cann't do alout of things grown-ups do. **you cann't stay up and ~~we~~ watch t.v.**

4.......you can't go to baseball games. **can't watch your programs.** can't drive a car. [5—11]

4.......I'm always too young. **I Have to come in a 9 oclock. I can't watch certain programs** [6— 11]

4.......Being picked by parents, not being able to go to the movies every weekend and **not being to watch good T.V. Show like The Great Escape, The Wolfman, Gay Purr-ee etc.** [6—?]

4.......Every grownup tells you what to do. You have to go to school. **You can't wath the shows you want to watch.**
Any further comments? Yes! You been waiting for your birthday for ten years and you still don't get it. **You can't watch t.v. late** [5—11]

4.......You usually don't go out, you're cooped up in the house. **I have to do to bed early. I can't watch television unless my mom**$^{or}_{dad}$**says I can.**
Any further comments? That's about all that's wrong. [6—11]

4.......**they pull you to bed rley do'nt let you wahct stary trak** I haet math [3—8]

4.......Nobody understands that things have changed. Your supposed to do what your parent say not what they do. **They don't understand that if you stay up to see your favorite T.V. show for another half hour isn't**
Any further comments? **NO.** **going to kill you** [5—10]

Just two more from this section of the questionnaires and the TV set gets turned off. A boy, 9: **Parents don't let you watch what you want to watch on T.V.** A girl, ageless and gradeless: *I get spanked from my dad with a stick.* **I can't watch T.V. at 8:00 I have to go to bed.**

There's no consensus on what constitutes a "late" or "early" bedtime. Various children specify virtually every hour or half-hour from 6:00 p.m. on through the late, late show as a good time *not* to have to go to bed. As for TV —and we have tried to relay the bulk of the children's references to it—our group reports it as another instance of grownups' interference with, and rules for, the conduct of young lives: **They command the TV.** Omitted were some

135

references to **horror movies** because it wasn't clear whether this preferred entertainment had been viewed in The Tube or the movie house or the drive-in. Children's affinity for just "the movies" is reaffirmed for us oldsters in complaints about **They don't let us go** (or **take us**) **to enough movies.**

What programs do kids like least to have their grownups turn off? Three children clue us in on five specific shows. To these one of them adds, **"etc."**—meaning *more* of those grim fairy tales television spins? When age 12 says, **"a special show,"** is it a network "special" or a favorite among "my programs?"

From Fifth Grade: **They don't like me to watch the pop groups.**

From Third Grade: I hate school. I hate to make my bed. **I hate to wach foat ball.**

A nugget for those concerned with television's influence† on the young cropped up in a response to Question 1 on a form without comment on either bedtime or tube-time. An Age 11, he or she, deposes . . .

They sit when you are putting away the Dishes.
They always think because they're older they can rule you.
They don't like you to say "you rang" when they call you.

Now wouldn't it be groovy to report that this is the same child quoted on page 20: **They can't take a joke!** Not so, sad to say, and with sympathy for a young one rebuffed for trying to jolly up his own *ménage* with a touch of *The Addams Family's* horrifically cheerful home life.

Does anybody get the feeling that, if television should suddenly cease to be, these children would not long miss nor mourn it? Consider that other controversial "influence" on children, the comics. Exactly two of 1,200 boys and girls mention them; of these, one is a promise not to read a **comicl book** to children when he or she grows up.

On the pressure gauge of dissatisfaction over bedtimes, with or without TV, early-to-rise registers a moderate calibration, quantitatively speaking. But it galls kids nonetheless to have some grownup **wake** [you] **up at the "crack of dawn"** or **pull the bedclothes off you,** and especially when **They make you get up early and go**—where else?—**to school.**

†Statistically, culturally, and educationally explored in pages 498-535 of "Television: A Selection of Readings from TV Guide Magazine" edited by Barry G. Cole (1970, New York, The Free Press); pages 95-112, "Sons and Daughters of Mom" by Philip Wylie (1971, New York, Doubleday & Company, Inc.); and "Big Bird, Meet Dick and Jane," a Critique of Sesame Street by John Holt (The Atlantic, May, 1971).

CHAPTER X

GHETTO KIDS

List three things you promise you won't say or do to kids when you grow up.

a) *the Devil [...]*

b) *or Curse*

c) *Hit [...]*

List three things which really trouble you about being a child.

a) *being teased*

b) *When I walk people step on my toe*

c)

Any further comments? *When children give me something I will say thank you dear*

Your Grade: **3**, Your Age: **8**,

"HAVE TRIED to get some ghetto kids, which should be interesting," said, in part, the letter heralding the arrival of some 40 questionnaires out of Third and Fourth grades, plus one from Sixth, in a city school. Examined separately, their distinguishing characteristic is an eye-catching brevity—no overflowing questionnaires here, though more children than not answered all the questions. Joined to, and looked at together with the whole body of replies, they most closely resemble groups reporting in from deep farm country. Ages eight to eleven are represented. Except for two boys and a girl who signed their sheets, there's no sex differentiation except by inference. Is it a boy or a girl who scrawls . . .

a) **y e l l**
b) **r o b**
c) **p e r s o n a l**

. . . in answer to Question 1, and no more except [Grade] **6**; [Age] **11**? Three Age 10s, Fourth Grade, can be set side by side, like this:

1.a)	**they maed me sick**	**alway fighting**	**I lro noit liKe to be hoiller at**
2.a)	**I will holler**		**I will**
3.a)		**B a d w o r d s**	
b)		**beat**	

Adopting this side-by-side format permits pairing up some kids of few words with their more talkative schoolmates. To do this it's necessary to modify our imitation of their handwriting, particularly the wide spacing between words.

From Third Grade, ages 9 and 8:

List the things that bother you most about grownups.

1.a)	m e e n	They yell at you.
b)		They dount let you stop and play
c)		They embarrassyou

List three things you will always remember to do around children when you grow u

2.a)	be kind	Let them go out side.
b)		Help them.
c)		Play with thim.

List three things you promise you won't say or do to kids when you grow up.

3.a)	shake	Bad wrouds.
b)	curse	Talk about outher peple.
c)	spake	yell at someone.

List three things which really bother you about being a child.

4.a)	spakings	you get bet up.
b)		cilden chase you.
c)		you get in trubl

Any further comments? no   I do not like glonups when thay tune
                         you upside down.

Two more 8-year-olds, likewise in Third Grade:

1.a)	they yell at you.	drinking yell
b)	they beat you.	walking down the street drinking
c)	tell you to do to much.	do not hit
2.a)		take care of them
b)		to ching when they do something in there driper
c)		I will then with you when you go some where
3.a)	don't curse	do not curse
b)	don't shake them.	do not smoke
c)	don't beat them.	do not give them a punishment
4.a)	they want you to do	do not pee in the bed
b)	something	do whene you whent to go to the bathroom
c)		you go

Ages 10 and 9 in Third Grade:

1.a)	Nothingbeat us	They think they can boss us around.
b)	tly allwasy	They get drunk to much.
c)		They say bad words around us kids.

2.a)	curse go out the road	I will always them through sick and Health.
b)	to do bad thing good	I will care for the poor children.
c)	curse	I will buy food, clothing for the poor.
3.a)	kind to my sister	I will never tell that their father said to come home with me.
b)	Be good to her	I will not say bad words to kids.
c)	curse	I will never chase them after school.
4.a)	Mother take care for me	Grownups have more fun
b)	Keep my slife tide	We have to go to bed early and grownups don't have to.
c)		Grown ups get to buy stuff that we don't want to eat.
Further comments? **Nothing**	I	

In the left-hand column, above, are some words in light-weight type, fragments of lines the child wrote first, then erased. The following are Fourth and Third Grade questionnaires by ages 10 and 8, whom we guess to be girls:

1.a)	When they have mucis	When she yell at me
b)	on we acn not sleep	When she make me go to bed early
c)		When she make me go to the store all the time
2.a)	Make them behave	to bring them with you when you go out
b)	don't let them fight	to buy them ice cream
c)		to buy them clothes
3.a)	Bad words	to not drink
b)		to not go to bed and let them stay up
c)		to not go out and leave them hom
4.a)	I don't get pretty dresss	When I can't go with my mother and father
b)		When I have to dry dish
c)		When I have to make up my mother
Any further comments?		when I have to comb it
		when I have to work
		when I have to

From Fourth Grade, ages 10 and 10½:

1.a)	They holler at you	you have to do what they say
b)		they make you wear what you don't want to wear
c)		And they always say how bad we are
2.a)	I am go to be nice.	learn to respect children
b)		watch your language around them
c)		and won't smoke around them
3.a)	Say bad words.	won't use bad language
b)	push the around.	won't drink alcahall around them
c)	hit on them all the time.	and won't smoke around them
4.a)	[Continued on next page]	

139

4.a)	go to school	you can't go places with you parents and you
b)	stay home all^{the}time	have to do what they say and they tell you to
c)	some are bad	come in the house even [if] your have fun
Any further comments?		I like grown ups who are nice kind and explain
		things to you when you have trouble

Both the following are 11-year-olds in Fourth Grade:

1.a)	grow - ups you eat	They beat you when you do nothing
b)		They make you do lots of things
c)		They make you stay in the house
2.a)	I will make the	be good to them
b)	children Eat	talk nice to them
c)		give them things
3.a)	Make the children to bed	I will not beat up little childrens
b)		I will not holler at other childrens
c)		I will not swar at them
4.a)	you will have to go	come in the house early
b)	to bed	go to be early
c c)		Do not holler in the house
Any further comments?		My Mother and othe people SURE teach
I like grown ups to		childrens to be Kind other people and do
be Good like Children		not backtalk to grown ups

Two examples of full (almost) to overflowing questionnaires from this particular environmental group are, first, one from a Master Age 9½ in Third Grade. He is one of those who signed his name:

1.a)	they boss you around too much.
b)	they talk about things that are personal.
c)	they make you go to bed early.
2.a)	be polite to when you speak to them.
b)	Set a good example for them.
c c)	Play with them when they ask you to.
3.a)	I will remember not to say bad words.
b)	not to yell at them.
c)	never smoke in the room when the baby is asleep.
4.a)	you have to do too much work.
b)	or when my nother or father die.
c)	when will somebody bother me or fight me.
Any further comments?	When I grow up and be a daddy. I will go
to work and earn money and have a good happy family.

The final example, a Fourth Grade boy or girl, 10:

List the things that bother you most about grown-ups.

a) They yell at littler children

b) They punishment you for nother

c) They alway hate people

List three things you will always remember to do around children when you grow up.

a) You will love them not hate

b) don't punishment them for even bad thing

c) Or don't hurt them

List three things you promise you won't say or do to kids when you grow up.

a) do not curse at them

b) do not hate them

c) do not beg them to do these or that

List three things which really trouble you about being a child.

a) people kill you

b) Your mother whip you ever day

c) Sometime your Mother and father hate you each day

Any further comments? Pleaes remember not to cures when you are body not to cures at children

Your Grade: 3   Your Age: 10

1.a) Some grown-ups kill other people
  b) Some grown-ups spoil some of their kids
  c) Some grown-ups dont listen to their kids and then they ask you why didn't you tell me

2.a) show them to be nice to others
  b) and act what you are
  c) not to fight and love one another

3.a) swear, holler
  b) talk about them
  c) I wont push them around and boss them

4.a) other older people think they king or queen
  b) and call you kids
  c) And say your to small to play go home kid

Any further comments?   **I like Grown - ups Who make me understand things better. I like to have Grown - ups like Mrs. W------- Whomakes me understand better things And spen more time with me**

A tabulation of these questionnaires showed rough handling (*beat, hit, kick, punch, push, shake, slap, spank*) to be the children's No. 1.a) "bother," and first among their "we won'ts" for future conduct. Add *punishment* and the preponderance increases markedly. This is where the previously quoted **strip you with belt** came from. A 10-year-old promises to **Don't! Beat them with a iron cord.**

Yelling, hollering by grownups comes next as "bother." Now add *swearing, cursing, bad words,* from the what-we-won't-do-or-say sections. Does it then surprise you that more than half of these children will remember to be *nice, kind,* and *polite* when they grow up, and to **set a good example**? One could add a small percentage resolving to help and care for children.

Their other gripes parallel those we've already read about through nine chapters. These kids' main troubles are likewise being bossed around, early-to-bed, and chores, in the general pattern. Conspicuously few are references to cars and driving, clothes, allowance, dating, can't have things, the telephone, television (one), movies—perhaps because there's no yakking clutch of Fifth and Sixth Graders on the scene. Or, are we here in territory governed by different rules?

More kids resolve not to drink than are bothered by grownups' drinking. Two say they won't smoke. Regarding school, three groan about having to go, one is borderline, two others positively gung ho. Yes, our **times table** enthusiast and the one who likes the **vice princala** are ghetto kids!

The concluding quotations are at random, as space allows, from children's comments that cross statistical lines:

2.a) **To keep clean**
  b) **To wash good**
  c) **To help others**

2.a) **watch out**
  b) **make sure they are kind**
  c) **never chase them**

4.a) **you can't were highheals**

4.a) **Not go swimming in the summer**
  b) **or not go to go to school**†
  c) **and not go to stay wiht people in the summer**

---

†Ambiguous? At first glance, we thought so and called it a "borderline" expression of interest in school. Read in conjunction with this 8-year-old's other troubles, it is the most outright declaration we have of a child's fear that he or she may be deprived of school.

1. killing   fighting   rob banks
2. help them   take good care of them   teach them too do right
3. not to hurt them   not to kill them   not to hit them
4. to bother dogs   to kill little things   to hurt fish

1.a) go to work
  b) bring home money
  c) do a good job
4.a) I cant get mony

3.a) you should go home   and change clothes uh
  b) your hair is nappy little girl
  c) Look at you shoes boy you new ones

2.a) be kind to them.
  b) Coth them.
  c) Feed them.
3.a) don't cuse in their Face.
  b) don't slap them in their Face.
  c) don't never ever drink in their Face.

2.a) have recpect for them
  b) wont spoil them
  c) let them get rest

"I hate to be a child," says the extrabold printing of an Age 10 in the "further comments" section of one sheet. But the "stopper," visually, of them all was the sign-off on a form from one who scrawls . . .

3.a) punch them.
  b) kick them.
  c) eat them.
4.a) you get a Beiting.
  b) you Dont get what u whant.
  c) you Be to mean.

. . . and then—

Any further comments? *yes what*

Help me. o Boy o Boy oo Boy.

Your Grade: **3** Your Age: **10**

143

They always look at me, when someone else is making the noise

They always laugh at me.

It seems to me, that all they want kids for, is to ~~scream~~ at ~~them~~.

Be sure to punish the bad child, and not the good one

Smile, then, you will make the children feel better

Not to be bossy.

Be mean.

Be mad

Hurt a child if he or she didn't do any-thing ~~wrong, or bad~~.

You have to worry about homework

You have to do work,

You have to have enough money to go ~~here, or there~~. They embarrass me the most when they laugh at me, or all stare at me when I dance.

5   II

Without including the 44 questionnaires discussed in the last chapter, 92 per cent attendance is the children's score in answering Questions 2 and 3. Only 24 had no ideas on what they will remember to do. 48 skipped, or never arrived at, Question 3. The "dropouts," omitting both, number a modest 31. A splinter group, just a sliver in fact, promised, **"I'm not promising anything!"**

144

CHAPTER XI

WHAT WE'LL REMEMBER TO DO AROUND KIDS
WHEN WE GROW UP

List three things you will always remember to do around c
grow up.

a) *I won't drink*

b) *I won't smoke*

c) *I won't talk about my kids*

List three things you promise you won't say or do to kids

a) *I will play with them*

b) *I will help them with homework*

c) *I will play jump rope with them*

JUMP ROPE, anybody? Oh, to be a *non*-grownup again, and *able* to join in
without collapsing the lungs and buckling at the knees! Without a thought for
her own time to come, a Miss Age 9, author of the words above, sensibly resolved to play with children when she grows up. If she follows her own advice
—no drink, no smoke—she'll be able to keep that promise better than most.

But the prime reason for isolating and displaying this portion of a questionnaire is to demonstrate—and warn—that two-way traffic between Questions 2 and 3 is rife. Observe the arrows saying, in effect, "Wrong way. Go
back," like those corrective signs planted on complicated highway cloverleafs
for the benefit of daydreaming (or nearsighted or bewildered or tipsy) drivers.

The directives on the forms are: Question 2—what will you remember to
do? Question 3—what do you promise to *do* or *say?* Now, to a child intent on
articulating his thoughts about **"stufe"** like this—perhaps for the first time in
his life—what's the distinction? If he's been *spanked*, simple: a grownup has
done something to him. When he's been *scolded*, he's been *done* to AND
talked at, or *yelled* at or *hollered* at. A combination of *doing* and *dinning*, so
to speak, that can be both discomforting and disconcerting. Thus, with gleeful
disregard for grownups' organizational expertise, many kids just said what
they thought when they thought it!

The children contribute about 6,000 lines of comment—practically a
bookful—in reply to the two questions on which we now focus. This chapter

concentrates on what they say they'll remember or promise to *do*. Though the kids may ignore our guidelines on subject matter, they're positive enough about "I will" or "I won't" behave. This is the way a Sixth Grader made sure she wouldn't be misunderstood:

List three things you will always remember to do around children when you grow up.

I'll
a) **Act adult.**
b) **think before I'll give an answer.**
c)

List three things you promise you won't say or do to kids when you grow up.

I won't
a) **Punish them hardly.**
b) **Tell lies.**
c)

. . . and we'll occasionally copy her method of avoiding confusion. The first group to be quoted is a selection of resolves, briefly stated, that appear over and over again.

I will be nice. I will care for them. I will help them.

I will not hit them. I will not say mean things to them. I will not bother them.

be nice   do not hit them   do not holer at them
I won't hit them   I won't holer at them   I won't sceem at them

I   will   play   with   them.
I   will   take   care   of   them.
I   will   be   good   to   them.

I will **be kind   be helpful   not grouchy**
I won't make them eat everything on their plate Yell at them Slap them

To be kind to them. To like them. To be very good them.

Dote be mean   Be nice to them   Dote play mean tick on them
Dote to lick them   Dote leave them at home

I will **be nice   buy them candy bars.   play with them.**
I won't **be mean   be impolite   play mean tricks on them.**

Be very good to them. Don't make them cry. Rock them to sleep.
Not to hit them. Not to kick. Not to be ugly to them.

Be nice   Share   No puaking

I will **Talk nice to people they are near. Be nice to them. Give them candy sometimes.**

I will not push. I will not lie to kids. I will be as good as I can.

Thus, in general, do the younger ones hold forth. Certain themes move right on up into Fourth, Fifth, and Sixth Grade territory. Out of more than a hundred one-line or "short" forms this blueprint of the future emerges:

I will **Be nice to them** (12)
Be nice (10)
treat them nicely (3)
Be nice and kind (2)
Be nice and kind to them
be nice to my children
be nice and ceourtious
Be nice and not crabby
Always talk nice
Be real nice to them
Be nice but don't spoil them
Nice

See also page 71. To continue . . .

Be kind (8)
Be kind to them (5)
Be kind to every child
be kind sometimes and maybe strik other times
treat them kindly
Teach them to be kind, thoughtful
Be kind, generous
kind

The short-spoken ones are 22 percent in favor of . . .

Be polite (11)
Act polite
I would be polite
Don't be unpolite
Be polite and let the children talk
Well Ill help them play sports and be polite to other adults
have polite manners
Teach them manners
mind your maner and not be bad
To teach them manners
Teach them good manners
I'll use manners
I will have good manners
Show them good manners
Have manners and be an example

List three things you will always remember to do around children when you grow up.

a) When you grow up ~~to meet~~ What you should know how to take care

b) if you smoke you keep smokes away from them

c) when they start to crall try not step on there hands

List three things you will always remember to do around children when you grow up.

a) I will let my kid. watch what ever they want to on T.V

b) I'll let them talk freely.

c) I'll try to stay calm when they do a small thing wrong

List three things you promise you won't say or do to kids when you grow up.

a) I won't spank kids, I'll think of something else.

b) I'll try not to ignore kids.

c) _____

List the things that bother you most about grown-ups.

a) When they jump to conclusions.

b) When they don't let you help with indoor work

c) When they treat you unfairly

List three things you will always remember to do around children when you grow up.

a) I will be fair to them.

b) I will not tease them.

c) _____

List three things you promise you won't say or do to kids when you grow up.

a) "I'm surprised at you."

b) "You don't try hard enough."

c) "Act your age."

List three things which really trouble you about being a child.

a) Not being old enough to do something

b) _____

c) _____

Any further comments? I think you were being rather personal, however I tried to help you with your book by answering the questions.

Your Town: _____ Your School: _____ Your Grade: 5 Your Age: 11

I will "set a good agzample for the smaller children," declares an Age 11, presumably, in his or her case, in a direction counter to grownups who **sometimes don't understand that you should be able to pick your own friends and sometimes expect you to do whatever they've planed for you to do without telling you about it.** Four others will **set good example** and/or **try to set a good example.** From two more: **tell them wright from wrong** and **teach them what is wrong.** A one-word resolve from one child is **help,** in the sense of . . .

I will **help them** (4)

    Help them when they need help (3)

    be helpful (2)

    help them with their school projects (2)

    help little children

    help them with projects, clubs, etc.

    Try to help them when they need it

    help them out

    help them in any way I can

    Have fun and go on trips with them is what one will remember to do. A simple **play with them** speaks out to us from four otherwise nearly empty questionnaires, but one of them includes [I will] **take them with me.** Where? To—

    Where they would like to go

    beaches, parks, movies

    let them tell places where they want to go

Some resolvers to be *polite, kind,* and *nice* specify further:

I will **not bother or embarrass them** (3)

    love them

    Be understanding   and be gentle

    act sweet   not to whip them

    be patient   be consistant

    Be sweet and gentle

    Try not to hert them. don't let them get hert

    Have them mind you, But don't be rough

    try to face there problems

    If I haved more things I'd give them it

    let them have freedom

    Never be on one side all the time

    not fool around

    Be friendly

    pay attention to them

    no bragging   not to show off

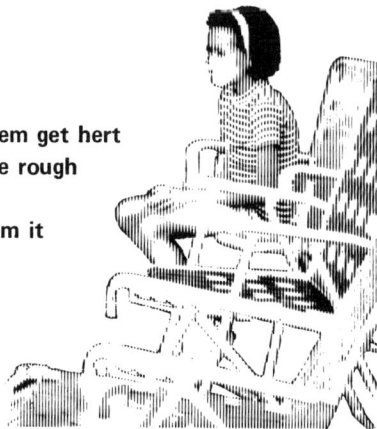

I will **Try to make them happy when their sad**
      be good   get a good job
      be intrested in what they do
      Have a good edjacation for them
      By all means bying nice to kids

Various ways and means of **bying nice,** with directives also from the set-an-example set, are . . .

> **Teach them to assume responsibility**
> **If they are my own make them mind me**
> **Try to smile at them**
> **Teach them games**
> **Act grown-up. Talk to children. Be sensible**
> **clean my own room**
> **treat them how you would want to be treated**
> **Remember to shut up when they want you to**
> **Showa good example to which they be like**
> **Have them be truthful**
> **don't say things that are not true**
> **Ansure questions turthfully**
> **Teach them to be good. Teach them not to lie**

An elaboration on the matter of truthfulness: Are you a girl? **No.** A boy? **Yes.** Your grade: **6.** Your age: **almost 12.** We've quoted him before (on page 79, top). He is bothered most by grownups because *(1.a)* **you explain two them about some things the best you** *(1.b)* **can and they don't get the right message** and (suddenly he's into *2.a*) **they lie and that it might become a habbit.**

      "**Tell the truth,**" says an Age 12 in Fifth Grade, adding . . .

I will **Watch out for them**
      Feed them will

From ages 9, 9, and 10:

> **Make them happy   keep promises**
> **care for them   take care of them   watch them**
> **love them   care for them   take care of them**

For all that they are so similar, the latter two lines originate from 900 miles apart. Speaking of **care for them,** here are suggestions on how to do it:

> **be understanding**
> **Disaplin them   Teach them thier religion and go to Church**
> **Make sure they are not lonely, have plenty of friends and have fun**
> **Trie to make them happy. Trie to please them. Trie not to get mad**

Be sure they don't play with matches. Make sure they don't go out in the street. Always say good-night
Keep them away from the road
Not to make them do things all the time
Try not to blow my temper and to get mad
if they are doing something wrong let them know about it
don't get married untill 21 or after
~~I Hold them~~ get the eggs. Feed them
encourage them

Turning now to what the kids promise *not* to do, the group quoted so far says, "I won't," emphatically to *beatings, hittings, spankings,* etc., nearly a tenth of them listing such treatment twice and three times. A favorite of ours is the line **I won't spank kids, I'll think of something else**—as punishment presumably, unless we're jumping to a conclusion, because *punishment* (the word) is not often used in conjunction with "violence" terminology. This supports Editor Greene's dictum: punishment may be deserved and thus not searingly resented; *methods* of punishment—or **for nothing**—are something else.

For the record, a tally of "I won'ts" establishes *yell* (etc.), *embarrass, set bad example, make fun of, be mean* and *call names,* and *baby them* and *spoil them* as main categories, with no decisive plurality for any one category.

Before quoting some of the more detailed questionnaires, hear just eight words, from one of the briefer forms, that sum up the mainstreams succinctly. We don't know age or grade, but we do know it's a boy who vows . . .

I won't make them ball their head off.

Let's award a good conduct medal in advance to a future father who may have endured, and will remember and recognize in his children, some of the high-tension climaxes when circumstances, grownups, sisters, brothers, other kids—even things like low barometric pressure and a cold coming on—reduce you to the point where there is nothing left to *do* but weep, nothing left to *say* but sobs. The trick, of course, is to distinguish between "bawl their head off" as a child's genuine "bother/trouble" and as a tactic effective in bringing grownups to heel.

In the following material, the excerpting is in the direction of developing additional details (as, I won't beat them **with a stick**) and some other currents of children's thinking ahead. Using *italics* to identify the *girls*, the arrangement is in order of ascending age.

Eights

I will never spit near children. I will not act like a crabby old woman around children.

I will not punish then inless they need it.

When I grow up I'll be a Mother.
I don't know what I'll be.
yes, I'll be a Mother.

I will **Play color read books right.**
Talk   go places.
Go to   the bech.
I Won't hert them.
I Wont play With them if they do'nt
Won't me to.

actgay and love them and try tobeas much like themasicould pos-
Could
sibley be and help them onceina While with there games.
there are alot of things and i can't eXplain them. p. s. never

I will **Put maches out of reach.**

Never give them everything they want.
I won't make my children sleep with a brother.

Nines

I will **Remember to give them their allowance.**
Tell them to wash before meals.
Teach them not to fight with someone smaller than them.
I will try not to lose my temper.
I will not put them to bed after 9:00
I will not say shut up to them

Cook good food for them. I Never tell my to stop play + work for
m
e
eat with silver waer. I won't gulp my food.

never hurt them bad
help them out
Get them glasses if they need then

Not to do anything dangerous. Not to act big.

Teach them the fire escape of the house   Be kind to them
Make them go to church
I won't let them play with Medicine
"   "   "   "   "   "   Matches
I won't let them fight

I will tell them the ten commandments.

N e v e r give them more than $ 1 0 . 0 0 a week n e v e r l e t
t h e m b e l a z y   never stop them doing wh a t they want

I will **Not to slurp in front of 1-2-3-4 year olds.**
Also not to do something bad in front of babys.
Also tell the truth.
I won't say SHUT-UP in front of children.
Beat them to death.

Don't give them any bad ideas. Give them a good ideas.

Don't to bother them about everything they do wrong.

I will **Let them go to the movie every once ofen.**
Let them go to the dump with me.
Let them go skating after school all nights.
Hit them at night if they fool.
I won't **Pull blankets off in the morning to wake.†**

Tens

I will *Keep my word in everything I say*
I won't *Threaten them*

I won't smoke. I won't drink. I'll try not to crash.

I will **Be fair, setting reasonable bed times, giving fair allowances, etc.**
Not make them do things they don't like
Don't ask embarrassing, and hard to answer questions like "Did you make any friends?"

I will **not let them play with fire. not shoot a gun. not take peoples things.**

I won't spoil them. I'll listen to what they say. I'll respect their rights.
I won't hit them too hard.
I won't say they are stupid when they try their best.
I won't make them stay in because they forgot to do something.

I will **To teach them the salfed rules.**
To help them with homework.
How to grow there own garden.
How to learn how to make a living.
To build their own homes.
To teach them their manners.

I won't *Give a little boy a bath. his Father can do it*

Don't punish them until you find out who did it.
Don't say you'll take things away from them when you say that just to scare them out of a habit or something.

I won't be nosy. I won't talk about how good I was.

† Source, a child living between 44 and 45 degrees N. latitude.

3.a) **Never say anything when you don't know what you**
a X) are talking about
B X) Don't teach them anything anlest you are sure

I won't argue with my husband.
I won't spank them unless I have a reason.

Won't be a wreckless driver. Don't run over one of the kids.

I won't insult them, laugh at them, be stingy. I'll be nice and won't
stare. These resolves are from an Age 10 who writes well, spells well, and appears to have at least *some* grownups well in hand, because **Whenever I've got**
them in a spot they switch the subject.

Elevens

From a Fifth Grade class, these two vehement one-line resolves—

I ~~Wo~~ WILL NOT BE MEAN!
I WON'T SPOIL THEM!!!!

—set a high-water mark for visual emphasis. Note in passing that, without further quotation, the children's agenda for future conduct could serve as ground
rules in observance of the Boy and Girl Scout Codes (as a glance at your cop-
ies of these will show). Now, some more instructions for being the perfect
grownup, by those who have never been one but will get to it soonest:

I won't kill or murder them. I won't take any L.S.D. I won't say any-
thing to them to hurt their feelings.

[I will] *Talk well about other people. Tell them to go as far as they can*
in school. Tell them that people usually judge them by the friends the[y] *keep*
so keep good friends. [I won't] *Smoke. Take LSD† or any other drug. Quit*
school.

Let them know you like them. Listen to their problems. Forgive them
if they ask to apologize.

I won't give them impossible chores to do

Not to give them hell so they won't cry.

I will not spank my kids with a wooden spoon past six years of age.

[I will] **give them a lot of food to eat and don't give sugar foods.** [I
won't] **hurt them cridictly.**

Not to fool around with sharp things [and] **show them fancy tricks**
with knives that they may get hurt on. [I won't] **tell them that your always**
welcome at a friends house. stand by and watch a little boy get beaten up by
a bigger boy.

---

† Making (with "I will not drink L.S.D." on page 9) three references in all to a specific
drug. Marijuana, zero.

List the things that bother you most about grown-ups. (What bugs you?)

a) They sort of boss you around!

b) ~~some~~ think their real neat!

c) That They have the right to boss us.

List three things you will always remember to do around children when you grow up.

a) I'am going to give them almost whatever they want

b) I'am never going to make them not me like

c) _or be mad at time._

List three things you promise you won't say or do to kids when you grow up.

a) I won't spank them with anything other than

b) I will won't have more then 4 kids. my hand

c) becouse you can't ~~talk to them~~ out sep'ratly

List three things which really trouble you about being a child.

a) That you can be bossed by grownups.

b) You have to go to sc hool!

c) Becouse you have to go where your parents go

Any further comments? I hope you have succes with your project!

Your Grade: 5 Your Age: 11½

I will give them some privacy! Understand them. Teach them to be neat. I'll trust them. I won't tell them a lie. Won't be hateful.

I will not kidnap.

[I won't] **talk about their skin color**

To treat them like thay are almost your age not a child. To let them have their say in things and not not listen to them because they're younger. Won't compare one child to another. Won't embarasse them. Won't tell them things that aren't true.

I promise never to overdo their punishment. I promise to lead them a good life.

[I will] Do some of the things to my children that my parents made me do. Make them eat the things they like.

play with them when they want to play. payatendion to them.

155

when hurt find out what's wrong make them learn their manners never yell because it doesn't help

[I won't] *Drink, and make them miserable.* [Say] *That there's something wrong with them to make them worry. Keep them "trapped up" in the house all day.*

[I will] **Give them special treats once in a while. I won't say they're too little to do this and that. I won't stop them from their play and tell them do** something else.

I will be myself and not act phoney

I will not say to go and pay someone back for what they did to them

When I talk to them I will treat them like a intelligent person. I will think they are *responsible but I won't make them too responsible. I won't talk about their faults behind their backs. Hug them in front of their friends. Make a dirty deal with an innocent child.*

Try to do things to help but not interfear. I won't tell them to much about my past troubles. I won't always set an example of myself. I do things wrong!

Let them be able to talk freely without feeling guilty.

I won't be a tattle-tale all the time. Not skunk the little kids in a marble game.

I will never make them think I know everything. Let them go on dates when old enough.

Give them some money ones in a while. Not make them go out on dates till they are over 16.

If one child is bad I won't make another be punished too.

I will not have a tantrum in front of them.

When I'm big I'll be nice to kids. After all kids are nice to have. When there good.

Twelves

I will remember that once I was a child and I was treated like one. I will remember that children must be treated kindly not always shout- ing **I will remember that children are like we we're when we we're small.** at th

If they ask a question I won't tell them there to young to understand. I won't put pepper on their tonques. I won't beat them.

   a) [I will] **Give them a chance to express their ideas**
   ~~b~~) **without telling them they're terrible**
   ~~X~~) **without even hearing them**

      not ball them out when weire in a bad mood. not get mad when they say God.

If I scold a child (if its a young child) I will give a reason for my actions
Not just send them somewhere not knowing what he did wrong

[I will] wash the car

I won't talk to them about my life. (unless they ask)

I will ask their apinion
Make children feel as if they are needed
To treat them as equals

I won't Discuss the neighbors advantages or disadvantages
Recall their actions when they were babies
Tell college stories which are dull to children†

Any further comments? Why do adults assume an air of superiority
and look down on ~~people~~ children?

I won't lecture them on every little thing they do wrong.

Help them to understand things on earth

[I won't] Give them a bad envoirment. Kill them.

Not to ask my daughter Did he try to kiss you you say "No darn it all"

I won't pick one out of a group and talk sweet to him.
I will walk past a group of kids and not watch.
I won't make questionnaires.

Not to take away their rights. Not always say no to everything they ask
Make them help but in a polite way. Not to call them the baby of the family.
Give them ideas what to do if you want to get them out of the house. If their
watching a show don't interupt because you don't like to be.

At least <u>try</u> to understand them.

lestin to what they are saying and don't walk away. never walk away
when they are crying.

I would ALWAYS tell the truth

[I won't] About Santa

I will *Explain to them why I do the things I do to them ex. scold them.*
Let them do the things they want to do within reason.
Treat them as my equel.
I won't act like a goody-goody.
I won't as them questions ~~than~~ about thing that don't really want to know about.
I won't deny them their priviacy.

Not to be hostile and put them in the spot. Not make fools out of them.

† "If parents would only realize how they bore their children!"—George Bernard Shaw,
"Misalliance," Episode I.

help them not <u>do</u> <u>for</u> them. help them have an independent mind. be fair in what do with them, work, play etc. punish with purpose. try not to punish phiscally.

[I won't] *whip the kids with the stick or whip*
Not to hit them if I am not shour they did it

not to promise them anything that you havn't got or will not get.

"Encorage learning," exhorts one, "Possess wide interests. Be an interesting conversationalist." If this sounds like egghead talk, no wonder! The author, Age 10, has made it through Sixth Grade in spite of grownups' **interests in trivialities, coffee breaks, abuse authority,** and giving away to emotion, as **When I leave friends' homes their mothers** ∧ **Kiss me.** (Uck.—*Ed.*)

sometimes

One of us has confessed (page vi) that the things he vowed to do as a grownup were all but one forgotten. What odds, therefore, that this new generation will do better? For the sake of a yet later generation let's hope that reasonable resolves like these get kept! . . .

I promise not to knock them around the room for 20 minutes.
I promise I will knock them for 10.

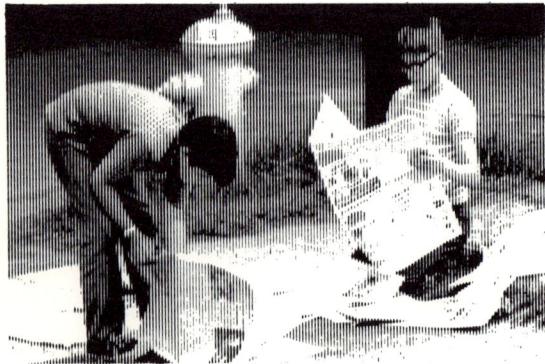

CHAPTER XII

THE SOUND OF GROWNUPS

Understanding grown-ups is hard!
The things they say!

THE THINGS they say—and that young ones remember! Grownups and literature itself deserve by now a "Bright Sayings of Grownups" compiled and edited by children. Perhaps some editor-publisher prodigy aged eight-to-twelve years some day will provide it. Meanwhile, this book performs the same public service rendered by its checklists of **unfavorite things** and **icky food** with a handy roster of grownups' conversation-stoppers without (to excess) repeating lines heretofore quoted or reproduced. Since the order of listing is random, you should know that the gambits **"How you've grown!" "Shut up!!!"** and just plain **"NO"** are quantitatively out in front, followed by variations on the themes . . .

"Get out of here"
    of my way"
    of this room"
    of here and stop bothering me!"
    of this house you're not wanted here"

"Go to your room"
    to bed without supper"
    clean your room"
    live somewhere else"
    jump in the lake"

"Oh, the little darling!"
    what a sweet boy or girl you are!"
    why did you cut off those beautiful braids!"
    you look just like so + so when it was your age!"

"Gee, your dumb!"
    you're the baby!"

Blush as one may over one's inadvertent slippage into this vernacular, it is not the stuff to give the troops; kids want it wiped out. Our young ones also

159

recorded with varying degrees of scorn the ensuing tidbits of dialogue from sources not only adult but **some big guys thing their so great.**

"You've grown like a weed"	"You can't go"
"When are you going to grow up?"	"Do your homework"
"Give all your money you have to me"	"Run away"
"If you don't like it lump it"	"I told you so"
"Don't pick on my sweet child"	"Do you like school?"
"Who's your girl fread"	"Your too small"
"Why are you mad at him?"	"We won't hurt you"
"Pretty neat at school, are you"	"I hate you"
"I would like to kill you"	"I'm gonna kill you!"
"Not to look at the catalogue. Or Els"	"Don't enterup"
"Don't forget to take your bath"	"Now be careful"
"Remember to get to bed at 8:00"	"Your a little kid"
"Well when I was young"	"No you can't"

"Are you satisfied with your mark on the quiz?"
"Many kids would be happy to have what you have"
"Your not old enough to think for yourself" (Ha)
"No young lady" (when in the store I ask for something, she says)
"I'm too busy" (when they are just sitting and I want something, they say)
"My Baby!" (so called by parents when "your out of that age")
"Little" (when prefixed to boy's or girl's name, as: "little Billy")
"I havn't seen you for so long" (when you have seen them just yesterday)
"I didn't promise anything!" (when reminded that they will buy something for me).

Kids say, **"Don't call bad names."** Some names they may have in mind are: You **brat.** You **punk.** You **queer.** You **fink.** You **idiot.**
Your a **devil.** You **sonofabeh.** You **seven year itch.**
My Mom call me penter and hunter.
My parents call me bugy boo pom pom.
My dad calls my cat "Biloomin George"

Probably dad's only teasing, but cats and ten-year-olds may not always get the drift. Nor does it strike us that age eight is equipped to quip back at...

You	**think**	**your**	**so**	**big.**	**get**	**out**	**of**	**the**	**bath-**
Your		**so**		**fat.**	**room.**		**get**	**your**	**but**
You	**are**	**a**		**pig.**	**out**	**of**		**the**	**food.**

A boy, 10, whose 2.b) resolve is to **Let them explain** (<u>**then** get mad</u>), promises *a)-b)-c)* not to say...

No buts   big words (unless they want them)   little boy/girl

... and another vows to **never say wise cracks.** Boy, 10½: **Don't say that they** are sweet, darling or lovelike when their friends are around. Boy, 11: **I won't say promises I can't keep.** Girl, 10: **I wouldn't argue about money.**

Some of our children's children will be the beneficiaries of such courtesies as: [I will] **say quiet instead of shut up . . . Always thank them if they give you things . . . When they draw something or make something I'll say it's good.** [I would] **say I love you . . . Be polite.**

Others will be precautionary in these words: [I will] **tell them never to get in peopls cars . . . Talk well about people . . . Never say anything they might repeat.**

Dutifully answering Question 3, most of the children talk about talking in terms of "I won't" and equivalent phrases:

I won't say   **I don't love them**
               I wish I din't have any kids
               which child I like better
               wrong things about them
               they're ugly
               I haet them
               they are cry babies
               they don't show respect
               they are stupid or slow learners
               I won't give them candy
               how they look
               it's grown-ups hour
               they cannot play with me in the gym, etc.
               to work outside for a couple of hours
               anything that will make them mad
               anything that isn't necessary
I won't   **talk about business when they're around**
               get sassy with them
               tell them spooky stories so they won't do bad things
Not to   **say mean things to them**
               say I am a "great woman"
               make them say "I'm sorry"
               say you can't play today
               say you stupid kid
I wouldn't   **say anything about child apperance**
               tell them anything they shouldn't know
I will try never   **to say things that would embarrass them**
I will not   **say that when I was a kid I was perfect**
               talk "baby talk"
               say I am going to heard them
               say I am raning away

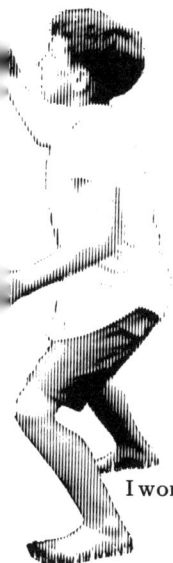

161

Smack in the middle of a questionnaire touching on yelling, restriction, **"they think you are coo-coo,"** homework, knee socks, shoving around, dates, and teeth (**I will check their teeth; I won't show them my teeth**) there is this emphatic pronouncement:

I will not say <u>damnit</u> to them.

"I hate myself," concludes this boy or girl, 9½, perhaps just having been downgraded from **feel wrong** to **feel worse**† by some grownup's verbal thunderclaps—which reverberate through the questionnaires in sons' and daughters' promises not to . . .

yell	swear	curse	say bad words
holler	sware	cures	say dirty words
shout	swaer	cuss	say nasty words
scream	swair	cuse	say bad language

List the things that bother you most about grown-ups.

a) *They don't understand me*

b) *Don't listen to me*

c) *Swear*

List three things you will always remember to do around children when you grow up.

a) *Be kind to them*

b) *Not to swear*

c)

List three things you promise you won't say or do to kids when you grow up.

a) *I won't swear at them*

b) *I won't say I did n want to kids*

c)

List three things that really trouble you about being a child.

a) *You have to go to bed early*

b) *You get yelled at from teacher*

c) *u can't do anything on your own*

Any further comments? *The parents hit you*
because they love you

Are you a boy? _____   Your Grade: *5* Your Age: *11*
Or Girl? *✓*

† See pages 72, 74

162

Even among questionnaires returned by children with little to say there were only two containing but a single word each. They read:

2.a)   **Do**   3.a)   **Swere**

... making a 50 percent showing "agin" bad language. 60 percent of the ghetto kids turned thumbs down to this, as did 21 out of 25 older boys and girls reporting in from an upper-grade classroom nearly 2,500 miles distant.

Curiously, this particular sound of grownups was not at all deafening in the children's lists of "what bothers us most," and—usually—it was put in as a second or third choice of evils, in this fashion:

don't holler	Smoking habits	They don't understand me
swear at me	Drinking habits	Don't listen to me
don't enbarrase me	Swearing habits	SweaR

spak us, swaer, be meen, talk to much, bals us

List the things that bother you most about grown-ups.

a) *They are quite unfare,*

b) *They rush me.*

c) *My mother calls me Markie?*

List three things you will always remember to do around children when you grow up.

a) *Be nice to them.*

b) *Don't bash them around.*

c) *Play tball with them.*

List three things you promise you won't say or do to kids when you grow up.

a) *I wont sware in front of them (if I SWARE AT ALL)*

b) *I wont smoke in front of them (if I do smoke at all)*

c) *I wont kill them for something I wont know ABOUT.*

List three things that really trouble you about being a child.

a) *I always get bashed around.*

b) *I'm never bragged about. And a kid needs it for*

c) *his Ego.*

Any further comments? *My mother and father think I'm a nobody. Because of the slightest bad marks in school. And so they bash me around some more.*

Your Grade: *6*   Your Age: *12*
Or Girl?____

Are you a boy? *yes*

163

Blaming things on me when I didn't do it.		They almost <u>always</u> smoke	
Swearing around little kids.		Some <u>drink</u> while driving	
Smoking and drinking around little children.		They <u>swear</u> a lot	

On actual count, these and equivalent Question 1 responses totaled less than 50, though all but a half-dozen followed up on profanity in Questions 2 and 3, as if to say: rough talk, this *really* bothers us most. Such responders were augmented by a bloc of "repeaters," those two-way traffickers between questions. Numbers, for once, are inadequate to the impact. The anvil-chorus intensity of **The things they say!** is something felt only in a run through all the questionnaires, reading this sort of thing on *every other page:*

2.*a)*	**Drive slow**	**Try to control my temper**	**be fair to all**
b)	**don't swair**	**Try not to swear**	**give them respect**
c)		**Try not to holler to much**	**not to cuss**
3.*a)*	**swair at them**	**Swear**	**cuss**
b)	**hit them**	**Understand my kids**	
c)		**Control temper**	

2.*a)*	**Not to swear**	**don't talk nasty**
b)	**Not to say nasty word**	**tell them about the facts of life**
c)	**Not to hit children**	**be considerate**
3.*a)*	**Not to hit children**	**swear at them**
b)	**Not to call they names**	**give them spankin's**
c)		**not let them go anywhere**

2.*a)*	**Not Swear**	**Take care of them.**	**be kind**
b)	**don't yell**	**Feed them.**	**use good words**
c)	**talk sweet**	**Send them to skoolol.**	**tell good storys**
3.*a)*	**Swear at them or**	**Do not swary.**	**not use bad words**
b)	**near them hit**	**Do not spank them.**	**not punch them**
c)	**them bug them**	**Do not say nanst worlds.**	

2.*a)*	**Have respect**	**Be nice**
b)	**Show them manners**	**Not be nasty and talk bad words**
c)	**Watch the words you say**	**[Not] Make bad impersions**
3.*a)*	**I will not talk to kids nasty**	**Beat** ~~them~~ ~~them~~ **on them**
b)	**I will not hit a kid**	**Say nasty words**

2.*a)*	**I will not swear.**	**Never leave matches around**	**I will not swar.**
b)	**I will act good.**	**Never swear**	**I will not talk nasty.**
3.*a)*	**I will not swear.**	**Never swear (they might reapet)**	**Don't talk fresh.**
b)	**I will not holler**		**Talk to them kind.**
c)	**at them.**		**Don't talk nasty.**

List the things that bother you most about grown-ups.

a) I think grown-ups are sometimes mean.

b) I think they fool you alot.

c) They make you do what you don't what to do like something that don't have to be done.

List three things you will always remember to do around children when you grow up.

a) I'll be nice

b) I won't hit them hard when they do something there not supos to do.

c) I'll go along with what they what to do that won't harm them.

List three things you promise you won't say or do to kids when you grow up.

a) I won't tell them things they should not know

b) I won't tell them bad things to make them dirty minded

c) I won't let them get a hold of a knive.

List three things that really trouble you about being a child.

a) You don't get as many things as your sister does.

b) You don't get to do the things or go where you sister.

c) You have to do the dishes when your sister is out playing.

Any further comments? When I'm around children I won't smoke or drink but I don't smoke or drink because its a trouble thing.

List the things that bother you most about grown-ups.

a) When some visotors come my father yells at me

b) most of the time, They hit you when you

c) dont mean it. And when he has guests he swears at at

List three things you will always remember to do around children when you grow up.

a) I will always hit them when they don't

b) mean it. I will always swear and yell

c) when visitors come

List three things you promise you won't say or do to kids when you grow up.

a) I will realy try not to hit

b) and I will try not toss in front of them

c) and when they get bigger I hope they don't do bad things

List three things that really trouble you about being a child.

a) Well your father tells you what to do

b) And when you don't do it you go in bed

c) So I try to do things write

Any further comments? And my father yelled at me so often that I felt like running away.

Are you a boy? ✓

Your Grade: 4 Your Age: 10
Or Girl? ___

2.a)	Don't hit them	Be nice	1. to watch when they play.
b)	Make them behave	Don't curss	2. make sure they bathe every day.
c)	not to swear	Act normal	3. swear.
			4. keep poison up high.
3.a)	swear	Whip them	1. swearing.
b)	hit them hard	curese to them	2. smoking.
c)	Not to make them to be perfect	Get mad at them	3. dvorceing.
			4. drinking.

The double four-part reply, above, is one of our few questionnaires that refer to divorce. From the same source another four-item reply is the only one that mentions gambling:

[I won't] **a. Swear b. Gamble c. Smoke or drink d. or argue**

The numbering and lettering are the children's own, as illustrated on

---

List the things that bother you most about grown-ups.

a) They think there are being even d

b) if they are wrong

c) They saw bad thing about you.

List three things you will always remember to do around children when you grow up.

a) Never teach them bad habits

b) Admit I'm wrong

c) Never embarrass them in front friends ect.

List three things you promise you won't say or do to kids when you grow up.

a) Never say bad things.

b) Never do dirty habits.

c) Never make them afraid of m.

List three things that really trouble you about being a child.

a) Being the oldest

b) Not being able to help my fam

c) or family. c) No' T.. treated my age..

Any further comments? Thanks for leting us express our feelings because grown-ups never care what kids think.

Are you a boy?_____   Your Grade: _ Your Age: 11
Or Girl? ✓

List the things that bother you most about grown-ups.

a) Our parents swear sometimes

b) say things about us we don't like

c) Holler at us a lot

List three things you will always remember to do around children when you grow up.

a) Be very kind to all small children

b) Don't do bad habits around them,

c) Don't swear around them so they will say those dirty words.

List three things you promise you won't say or do to kids when you grow up.

a) I won't swear at them

b) I won't make them embarrassed

c) I won't do unnecessary things

List three things which really trouble you about being a child.

a) You can't cook enough

b) Your mother won't let you sew

c) Your mother has to tell you what you have to wear to school.

Any further comments? I don't like some of the food at hot lunches, and your mother won't let you take cold lunch.

Your Grade: Five   Your Age: 11

---

page 40—where one of the reproductions is still another example of **swear, cuss** disapproval. To continue . . .

2.a) Set a good example for children.
  b) Listen to them at times. to see what thay have to say.
  c) Not to say bad words in front of them.

3.a) I won't sware in front of people.
  b) I will not hit or rally hurt any.
  c) Or scare them so they will be scared of that for life.

2.a) Not swear because it will teach other children to swear
  b) Not to punish them in front of people
  c) To always listen to what they have to say   before I punish them

3.a) Not to swear
  b) Not to call them names
  c) Not to punish them very bad

167

2. *a)* Not to sweare in front of them.
   b) Not to let them stay up late.
   c) Not to get in a lot of trouble.
3. *a)* Do not Sweare in front of then.
   b) Not to tell then dirdy jokes.
   c) Not to hit any one in front of then.

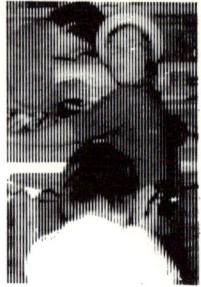

2. *a)* not to swear.
   b) not to whisper
   c) not to use big words.
3. *a)*   I will not swear.
   b)   I will allways remember to say please + <u>thank you.</u>
   c) I   will never get angry unless nessesary.

2. *a)* not to swear.
   b) or not to lie.
   c) and not to drink beer around them.
3. *a)* not to swear to them at all little or big.

2. *a)* not to swear around little children because they might say bad words
   b) be polite ! and nice to people.
3. *a)* when I grow up I will not swear or holler at them to much!

Tired of that word "swear?" The kids have forceful variants—and a number of them imparted to their questionnaires a sort of crescendo build-up to peak strength, in the manner of one Third Grader representative of both his/her contemporaries and elders. Hurt, kik, puch; not to kik, puch, hurt; always hit you, puch you, kik you—thus the rocky road of life for this one in three sections of questionnaire. It's written in a bigger and clearer hand than many, but he/she wrote biggest and clearest in promising . . .

Not to say durty wods.
Don't look at durty thins.
Do not show durty thins.

. . . with evidence of erasure and correction underneath the penciling to suggest that more time and thought was expended here than elsewhere. An eight-year-old quoted in the "big brother, big sister" pages (**sister's say not'y thing's**) voiced further disgust as follows:

2. *a)*   teach them go thing's
   b)   I will tell not say not'y thing
   c) don't play not'y thing
3. *a)* don't say nothing bad
   b)   teach them not to be bad
   c)   Do not steal

Thus, in terms other than s - - - -, a Miss Eight leading off:

I will **teach them to pray.**
teach them about growing up.
teach them not to say naughty words.
I won't **say words in vain.**
make them watch horror movies.
I won't let them sleep without praying.

I will never say things nasty.   do note say nassty things. †
I will play games with them.   do not   yell at them
I will be polite.
I will try not to get angry.   domote say nassty words.
I will not spank them.   arwnd people.
I will not say nasty things.

Never get real mad and say naughty things.
Talk right around them so they will learn to talk right.
Make a good example for them.
I won't real nasty with them

I will **Never to cuss.**   I will not say bad things
Be kind to them.   I will not say bad news
Pay lots of attention to them.
I won't say hell or damn it.

I will **not to talk about wrong words or things in front of them.**
not to tase then about their way's.
not to make the same mistake my folks did.
not to spoil them.
not to be sharshon them.
not to teach them bad words, bad things, and ways.

I will **talk good around your children.**   learn to respect children
do not shout at them to much.   watch your language around them
do not have a better lunch then them. and be kind to them
I won't **talk dirtye.**   won't use bad Language

I will **Not use bad language.**
Not to use bad manner.
Or not to teach a child to say dirty things about another perso.
I promise I will never be verry strict to a child, I will let the child do any
    thing that is right.
I promise never to use bad bad words in front of a child.

†Erased by Master or Miss Nine, then entered below as a proper 3.a) answer.

169

I will **Don't say bad or unruly words.**

Be nice and not smart.

Do things that make an good influience of them.

I won't call them bad names.

I won't hurt them.

I won't say words that make a bad influience.

Here are a concluding few quotes from the other hundreds of question-naires, brief ones that bore down on rough talk quite as emphatically:

Dirty words I will never say.

Not to say   nasytes word.

I will not say foul language around them.

I will always say pleasant things

I will never say (~~swears~~) nausty words

I won't say bad things or have a devors so my kids won't hear it.

Don't swear ever, not only in front of kids.

<u>**Never swear around them**</u>

I won't say bad words or things, because they would say them too.

I wouldn't swear in front of them or at any time.

I won't sware at them or none thing dirty

I won't **S W A R E**

say nastey words at them !

swear in front of them or anybody else as far as that goes.

I wont let any person make me swear in front of a person.

I will never will   never swear around children

[I promise I won't] **Always to fight**

                             Always to hate

                             always to cuess

don't swear because ladies ~~don't~~ aren't → sopposed to swear

don't cuse around them

I will not dress in front off them

Not to kuss at them

Not to hit a child to much

Don't   ask me any   more stupid ?ˢ Mr. Green or Qui e n

OK, young friend, enough. We've harped on the subject of bad language to the point of surfeit, but only because you and your colleagues do so, too, and so positively! Whereas, from time to time, you cushion your complaints by prefixing the word "sometimes," when you state your "wills" and won'ts" your qualifying words are apt to be "always" and "never." A girl, 12, nevertheless, did ease off on us a bit, like this . . .

Any further comments? **Sometime grown-ups get carried away, by making kids do dishes when they lay down or spank children with belts or anything dangerous and talk felthy.**

Also, it cheered us to hear from a small group resolving to **talk desently** in our native tongue:

2.a) **Use proper english.**   3.a) **Don't harm them.**
  b) **Don't swear.**   b) **Use proper english.**
  c) **Act proper.**   c) **Don't swear.**

**I will try to be nice
have good maners
use right English**

**I will tell them the truth about fairies, and Santa
I will give them good habit
I will try to speak proper English**

**I'll never lose my temper.
I'll try not to emberrass them.
I'll not use bad English.**

I will speak **Good English,   the Best I Can**
I won't speak **Bad English to them
Swear at them**

Yell, holler, scream. Swear, cuss, talk felthy. The sound of grownups, amplified. Is there—when grownups' voices pitch up to the levels of anger and reproach—some piercing, high-frequency sound that only a child can hear?

"Kids don't have to swear to be popular!"

List the things that bother you most about grown-ups.

a) Gettin mad at my brother or sister,

b) When they yell too much,

c) When they get mad at me becaus I try to help.

List three things you will always remember to do around children when you grow up.

a) I will remember to not be strict

b) I will remember to try to underst

c) I will remember to not sware,

List three things you promise you won't say or do to kids when you grow up.

a) I promise I wont talk meanly,

b) I promise I wont make them ea

c) or make them do work.

List three things which really trouble you about being a child.

a) Im troubled about staying back in s

b) about getting hit by mom or dad

c) about getting bad grades.

Any further comments? I wish grownups would not get so mad, but, I love they mom and dad.

Your Grade: **3** Your Age: **8-7**

CHAPTER XIII

" . . . JUST ONE MORE THING"

List the things that bother you most about grown-ups.

This is not my family →

a) *When grown-ups do something wrong they just laugh when i*

b) *Grown-ups think they own every thing.*

c) *Some grown-ups make you spend all your money on thing which you do not need.*

"YES, WHY do you ask these questions? You have to interfear in peoples business doen't you. I doen't see why you should. You just want to find out if children like there parents. Well I love my parents and you aren't going to find out mutch from me."

After thus blasting us for the Nosy Parkers we are, this Fifth Grader apparently decided that she'd better get rid of the **mutch** she'd already written in reply to Questions 1, 2, 3, 4. Before teacher collected her paper she had managed to erase lines 1.*a), b), c)* and 2.*a)* almost to obliteration. Editor's X-ray vision—rendered even more supermanageable by bifocals—pierced through, however, to a familiar trio of grievances: **Have to go to bed at 9:00 P. M. Don't let you do what you want. Have to do dishes.** So there, young lady! But we love you, too, especially for letting us know so resoundingly that love conquers all—yea, even unto dishwater!

Including forms in which there are no answers to Question 1, Question 4, or both (no news is good news, we always say), more than a hundred questionnaires suggest that **this is not my family** but somebody else's grownups giving the whole crowd a bad name.

With sentiments and punctuation so similar that one would think we're dealing not only with an example of collusion, but *twins*, two eight-year-old Third Graders proclaimed:

1.*a)*	**Gron-ups dont bother me.**	**grownups dont bother me.**
b)	**I like them.**	**I like them.**
c)	**They are nice to me.**	**they are good to me**
2.*a)*	**Do not push them**	**the same thing they did**
b)		
c)		
3.*a)*	**I will not say nasty wrods**	**I wont hurt them.**
b)	**at them**	
c)	**not to be strict**	
4.*a)*	**They dont bother me.**	**I am Happy the way I am.**
b)	**Im happy**	
Any further comments?		**nothing ! ! !**

Collusion, twins, or whatever, in this Third Grade† at least, grownups got a very fair shake. On page 38 were quoted three other expressions of love and loyalty to Mom and Dad, and here is still another from that same classroom. Speaking out of the pit of usual Third Grade woe, plus **They won't give me a cat,** a Master or Miss avows . . .

They drive me nuts. But I love them.

Already quoted is a Fourth Grader's **I think grownups are very nice.** An Age Nine, additionally bothered (puzzled?) because **Every Sundy my mother and father go to bed,** signs off:

. . . just one more thing I still love my mother and Father. And everyone

Age 9: Heading up an almost empty questionnaire:

Nothing bugs me about them.
If there were no parents we wouldn't be alive.
Nor would we have food, clothing, shelter, we have every thing to be thankful to parents.

Girl, 10: Steal, lie, and swear she will not do in future. For the present . . .

I like grownups and I try to be one
I an most of the time

Age 9: No bother or trouble but one: "I don't get to do all the grown-up things that I know I can do." Then he/she observes:

. . . Some parents only say good things about their children and treat them so special and don't care to much about other kids. Most parents do, care even about other kid.

---

†Reminder: Third Grade is least represented in the 1,200 forms, among them some of the ghetto kids, a silent (on the present subject) minority.

Girl 10: "I love being a kid."

I have a good mother.
I have a good Granmother
and a good Granfather.

Two *Age 11s:* Collectively won't cuss, be selfish, mean; will be nice, "not to fight" or say bad words. Concerning grownups:

1.a) **They don't bother me**   **They give you clothes.**
  b)   **And help you live.**
  c)   **Get you things.**
4.a) **Nothing bothers me being a child**

Boy, 11: Promises not to be an "old grouch," even though "when I miss 1 or 2 on a test, my father yells at me," and "My mother makes me do women's jobs." And yet . . .

    . . . I have a good family, and I'm glad my parents are who they are, and I know what they do, are for my own good. They want me to be a good person when I grow up.

Age ?: Scornful of "hippies with young children and smoking in front of them . . . And one friend's mother smokes when preparing food." Sometimes . . .

    I cry because I love my parents so much—and my sisters— and relitives . . . I guess I am just soft hearted.

Girl, 12: Promising "I will try to help other people as I hope they will do to me," devotes half her questionnaire to . . .

1.a) **My father drinks very much and it bothers me. I'm afraid he got to**
  b) **get in a reak. And when he drinks he picks constantly and I do love**
  c) **him very much.**
4.a) **There is nothing wrong about being a child I'm loved I'm feed, I'm**
  b) **well treated and colthed and I'm happy to have parents who love**
  c) **me.**

Girl 11: Oppressed by "Bigger people pick on you. When their around 18 or 19 they show off to much." But, most emphatically . . .

    My parents <u>are not</u> like that. <u>True</u>

    Here's a medley from Fifth and Sixth grades by kids whose gripes are among, or coequal with, the troubles and bothers bouncing around on pages 62-86 (which see):

    I am perfectly happy with my parents . . . Parents may scold a lot and stuff but they are doing it out of love I may say a lot of things that bother me

but I still love them . . . I'm glad I'm a child, I wish I could remain one Fortherestofmy liFe. When I get older and have childrenofmyown I willtreat them kindly . . . My parents don't consider me a child. I only mean people such as neighbors, some relatives and others. I'm an adult to my parents . . . Not all parents are wonderful, but mine are (I think) the best in the world . . . I don't have hardly anything against grown-ups. I love my parents and I love being a child . . . I'm too short. I keep getting beat up. I really don't mind it because it's fun. I think most adults let you do anything you want if it's proper. I think they are real nice to you . . . I like being a child you get work and play.

Dear Sir: [concludes a girl, 12]   I really can't think any thing that bothers me about grown-ups. I enjoy being a child, a child is young and that's the beauty of it all and it only comes once *in a lifetime!*

This is one who will remember always **to Love.** The girls outnumber the boys in wholehearted parent-appreciation as well as general satisfaction with the childhood condition. When it comes to praise-with-reservations, more boys join in:

1.a) **Well my parents don't bother me much.**
  b) **But I would like to have a little free time.**

        . . . In my opinion grownups do things for childrens own good. Wether its grounding us or helping us with our homework they try to help us. They do make mistakes though.

    I like my father and mother even if they are a lettle eggy once and a wile

      grown-ups aren't really bad.

    Not being able to go places   but maybe this is for my own good
    I also think that a grown-up scold you sometimes for your own good.

Scoring these almost love lyrics as a duet, we hear . . .

Yes, in a way I am glad that grown-ups boss me around and ball me out because I usually need it when I get it . . . **Parents may be strict but they are just trying to bring us up right . . .** *My parents are nice at times & sometimes they are saying do this & do that . . .* **In a way elders are trying to be the nices they can. The parents try there best . . .** *The parents hit you because they love you . . .* **I really do like being a child and grown-ups are'nt that bad . . .** *I think its nice being a child and this it want I'm going to say and be when I grow up . . .* **Grown-ups are not all that bad though. They teach you many things. They sort of guide you until you grow up . . .** *Most of the time parents are nice. They take you on trips. get nice clothes for you, make sure you get good*

grades, and most of all they teach you the wright things and they stear you in the right direction . . . **Yes, I like my father and mother in one way because they are building our new house and we can ride the ski-doo** . . . *Yes! I think most adults are very nice. But some are not* . . . **Sometimes they bother me, sometimes they don't. And for No. 3, I won't drink at all** . . . *Some grownups are mean and some are not* . . . **Sometimes grownups go to far with teasing and fooling around** . . . *But really I think that there isn't many things rotten about being a child* . . . **Yes, I think that parents and grown ups should be nicer to you. It is necessary to have nice parents and grown ups, it is better for life.** Thank you.

A girl, saying first that about the only thing that bothers her is **some treat you like a 5 year old when your ten or eleven,** wrote the following apt description of one of our civilization's cultural cycles:

I have a very happy homelife until the bills come in the mail.

A few, in putting grownups on probation, put in also some hints and helps on taking us off; the 10-to-12s were most willing in this respect:

[I will] **SET A GOOD EXAMPLE (LIKE MY PARENTS DO)**
[I won't] **CONFINE THEM TOO MUCH (IN YARD IS OK.–BUT IN** . . . **I hope something will become of this!!!**   **ROOM, NO!)**

. . . **I won't ever no matter what leave my little kids alone in the house when my wife is gone.**

. . . **grownups should make more kid work instead of play**

Try not to get divorsed.

. . . **Yes, I think you should get a better thing for us because we nead it**

When you grow-up you should chang your ways

One parent, it would seem, can get off probation by changing just *one* way: that insensitive tendency in grownups to fly off the handle. Her daughter, 12, bottomed-off a full sheet of Sixth Grade-type peeves and good intentions in this fashion:

Any further comments? **If my mother gets mad I have no say for my defense, she just yells and tells me what I've not done in the past 3 days.** *I Love my Mom*

I love my Mom, out there in the margin, had been toned down by erasure to a tint so pale that our X-ray vision missed it until the dozenth-or-so examination of the questionnaires.

But there was no missing the jam-packed questionnaire transcribed on the next page. It provided the artwork used to decorate the half-title and binding of this book.

List the things that bother you most about grownups.

(That means it's bad)

a) They say what they think of cuscin D-----.

They say, "When I was a little girl, I never did this,

b) or that, I was always good." Who do they think they are, George Washington?

c) They tell you to wash your hands when youve already done it twice.

List three things you will always remember to do around children when you grow up

a) Give them ice-cream instead of brussel sprouts.

b) Tell them to give me birthday presents.

c) Tell them to quit school.

List three things you promise you won't say or do to kids when you grow up.

a) Never kill them by watching the news.

b) Never give them Brussel Sprouts.

c) And I won't say, "Go wash your hands" when they have done it twice.

List three things which really trouble you about being a child.

a) I it's seems like I'm a servant.

b) There always seems like something's wrong with me.

c) Why can't I be a grown-up?

Any further comments? All these things said above are what I

might think, but I really truly love my parents, and I know

they love me too, even though they make a few (ahem!) mistakes.

CHAPTER XIV

A REPORT CARD ON ADULTS BY CHILDREN

TEACHERS REPORT This report is issued by the subject teacher as a supplement to the regular report card for the purpose of giving the home more detailed information about pupil's progress in the subject. The school will appreciate both comments and conferences if necessary. Please sign and return this report.

Teacher's Signature _____

CLASS ATTITUDE	EFFORT	CLASS PARTICIPATION
✓✓..Most acceptable	✓✓..Most acceptable	Oral Written Lab.
..........Good	..........Usually satisfactory	✓✓ ✓✓..........Excellent
.... Shows initiative	..........Fair	....Usually Satisfactory
..........Cooperative	..........Irregular at times	....Fair
..........Indifferent at times	..........Often poor	....Often
..........Inattentive at times	..........Very poor	Unsatisfactory
..........Backward in recitations	**PREPARATION of ASSIGNMENT**	..........Poor work because of absences
..........Uncooperative	✓✓..Always well done	..........Careless in following directions
..........Should volunteer more in class	..........Usually satisfactory	..........Not accurate
..........Should do more concentrated study at home	..........Often passed in late	..........Often does not get work done
..........Should get more help from teacher after school.	..........Incompletely done	
	..........Fairly satisfactory	
	..........Poorly done	
	..........Usually not done	

OTHER REMARKS *PARENTS HAVE A RIGHT TO KNOW HOW WELL THEIR CHILDREN ARE DOING, THEY SHOULD BE INFORMED ABOUT THEIR GOOD ACCOMPLISHMENTS AS WELL AS OTHER THINGS. FROM A TOTAL OF 70*

ONE OF THE cooperating teachers topped off his enthusiasm for this project, saying "it could serve as a good text for parents to evaluate what they are doing to their children." Thus, above, is a facsimile report card for guidance in marking one's own performance in parenthood or the performance of the genus Grownups, as registered in the questionnaires. Just change the word "CLASS" in the headings to read "HOME" or "FAMILY." Assume also that grownups as parents have passed elementary Biology and Breadwinning. What ratings do the kids give us now in, say, primary Home Economics, Life Style, and Guidance?

Anyone wishing to play this game either for keeps or for whimsy should stick with Editor Greene at age 13, and—Don't Overinterpret. Because:

First, the questionnaires are weighted on the side of "what's wrong." The kids were asked to complain, and they did. They cooperated, quite in the spirit of a Master or Miss Age 10's admonition: **I would never tell a child there not coaproating because I have never seen a child that didn't try.**

Next, every sideswipe at grownups in these pages is by a person who has never been one. For all their caterwauling about money, there was one — just one — child saying that he or she is bothered by grownups most because: **They have to pay bills.** [Yes.—Ed.] Consider, too, that when it suits his purpose, a child may think of "grown up" as anyone aged 13 on up.

Again, as Chapter XIII evidences, some boys and girls regard the childhood condition with equanimity and affection. Here's one who wants no part of the grown-up condition and the grown-up power that goes with it: **I don't want to be an adult because you have to boss little kids around. You have to tell them what to do.** From another Fifth Grader: **I'm not really complaining, but I would like to be an adult and be on top of things!**

Do he and like-minded friends have any notion of how many adults are *not* on top of things? For instance, Dr. Schroeder writes,† "I would estimate, from my acquaintances and my patients, that *90 percent* of people are bored by their jobs, which they have been forced to accept." From another source, "I don't mind working hard for a living, but I'll be damned if I really like being *scared* for a living."* Certainly the children sense that all is not necessarily pizzas and Coke in adultland, but we venture that not many are yet wise to the pressures that may drive a teacher to . . .

when one kid gets in trouble she bursed out mad at everybody around

. . . or that cause a parent to turn on them and say **!!†?+/*⚡!?††⚡!!!**

Difficult for children to comprehend (though our Chapter XIII group can perhaps give us the lie in this matter) is the parent's dilemma when, on having a request fired at him (to do, to get, to go), his heart says "yes" but his judgment—or his pocketbook, and eventually his mouth—says "no." When, on the second or third or tenth round, "no" becomes **"NO!"** all the reasons-why ever invented don't heal a child's disappointment. So we find certain "disadvantaged" ones naming their troubles as **not having a pool.** Or something. It doesn't help grownups either, in this kind of situation, to have to decide AT ONCE and in the presence of witnesses. Moreover, parents have to be on guard lest they paint themselves into a corner from which they hear their child lament: **They promised me a pony, but I didn't get it!**

"Sadness that underlies many of the replies"

THIS EFFECT, which recurs persistently throughout the questionnaires, was noted by the same teacher who recommended them for evaluation purposes, and he had access only to the batch of 54 that he sent in. These have already enriched our Chapters IV and V, but among them was none so tragic as the one shown on page 10, or disheartening, as . . .

1.a) **They think thier so tuff.**
 b) **They can hit us little kids and get away with it.**
 c) **They acuse you of things and they keep rubbing it in.**

†From the vantage of 35 years' medical practice and science; see page 11. Italics in the above quotations are ours.

*A successful competitor in the struggle to be (and stay) on top of things in the Detroit auto mill, quoted by Frank Rowsome, Jr., in "Think small. The story of those Volkswagen ads." (1970, Brattleboro, The Stephen Greene Press)

Any further comments? **They never spend money on you. I've got a father that is so chep he never spends money on us. I real don't like my father. My father and mother are divorced.**

These two extremes are: one from the country, the other from a community that can be labeled either "big town" or "small city." The ones that affected the teacher are by kids living in prosperous territory (and he should be gratified to know that it's a group with fewest complaints about **we half to go to school**) where one would least expect to find an aura of "underlying sadness." But . . .

> **They say they like your present, but they really don't**
> **Not spending enough time with you**
> **They make all the family choices about where to go**
> **Most don't have manners.**
> **It bugs me when grownups just sit and stare at me.**
> **You can't say what you feel to parents**
> **They have a way with revenge**
> **They broadcast things you don't want anybody to hear.**
> **I'm always bothered during something good**
> **They always comment when you do something differently** **then they do.**
> **They're never home when you need them.**

Amid the vociferousness of the questionnaires, this miscellaneous quieter comment builds its own atmosphere. It is gloomy. When the kids speak of laughter—not very often—it's usually in this vein . . .

> **When they laugh a lot and they don't tell you what their laughing at.**
> **laugh at me when I don't understand something**
> **I don't like being laughed at when I think I'm correct.**

We haven't emphasized enough that children feel sad and boggy when . . .

> **They always go out to dinner.**
> **They are always going to parties**
> **I can never go with my parents to parties**
> **when my mom says that we're going somewhere and I get ready and we don't**
> **You can't go out for supper with your wife.**

This boy's wording of his No. 1 Trouble struck as as a direct hit on what the trouble really is. Observing that grownups seem to have a good time, and occupy much time, in this kind of social activity, children would like, please, to have a bigger piece of this kind of action. Of pleasure and adventure shared, within reason. We can't turn the clock back to Longfellow, nor has "togetherness" worked to perfection, but a partial meshing of adults' "happy hours" with *The Children's Hour* would seem to be in order.

181

What's sad is the children's composite portrait of grownups who turn *themselves* off from a simple and rewarding pleasure—enjoyment of children!

But take it easy. Whatever bridgework goes into the generation gap had better follow the children's guidelines. **Don't act like Donald Duck.** Don't get carried away because kids can be **so-o-o-o cute!** Act your age, because **it is terrible to watch a grownup try to act like a kid.**

Future Ladies and—Gentlemen?

THE CHILDREN state loud and clear how they'll behave when they grow up. They will try to be decent. What's sad is the image they project of grownups who aren't. Even with assurances that **this is NOT my family** who **abuse authority** and **pick on us little kids,** our cumulative child's-eye-view of adult behavior is about as flattering as a comic strip.

Still, *someone* is setting an example for that "A" in Deportment they resolve to earn when they grow up. If they express exasperation toward many, they as yet have malice toward none. Boys and girls alike are sensitive to the qualities embodied in such words as *decent, sensible, reasonable, gentle,* and *courteous;* they use these words well. Some of the girls speak of being *ladies,* and *ladylike.* Is it significant that no boys use the word *gentleman?* Perhaps they've heard it noised around the playgrounds that nice guys don't win.

the End big mouth Stephen be a beer drinker

p.s.——→

Green

Postscript

Any further comments?   Thankyou for letting us come up and see how they make and do the machinery work. And make papers or magazines. Maybe we could come again by.^{name}A— B——

The Stephen Greene Press recently was host to a busload of Sixth Graders on a field-trip exploration of book publishing.† Because, in the interim between commencement and completion of this book its original 8-to-12-year-old authors had kept right on growing in spite of moon walks and other stuff, this opportunity to have some questionnaires filled out by a late, late panel of 11s and 12s was not to be missed. The chaperoning teachers (our thanks tendered herewith) obliged by taking away some blank forms for use when and if possible. Eventually, a dozen or so replies came back, from which we've transcribed the courteous bread-and-butter note appearing above.

Transcribed below, the briefest and lengthiest of the rest:

1.a) **They tell me to go and feed the dogs**
2.a) **I will be nice to them.**
3.a) **Slap them out.**
4.a) **You cant go to R—— and watch girls.**

1.a) **always saying take a bath.**
  b) **Don't listen to me.**
  c) **always making me eat eggs.**
  D) **alway telling me what to do.**
2.a) **always going to send them to bed before 12:0o, oclock**
  b) **going to let them go out doors**
  c) **going to be nice to them.**
3.a) **I won't say nasty words for them to learn**
  b) **won't call them names**
  c) **I won't spank them unless I have to.**
4.a) **can't stay up late**
  b) **can't go to the store**
  c) **can't use the kind of tooth paste I want.**
Any further comments? **can't Do any thing thier the**
       Boss. I the slave. they always say Do this + Do that
       But if I Don't, I get a spanking

---

†"Not to take them to uninteresting places (Unless especially educational)."—Boy, 11, in reply to Question 3.